*To my parents
Ronald and Annie Redmonds*

INTRODUCTION

The popularity of genealogy and family history as leisure pursuits has created a demand for reliable information about surname origins and history which cannot yet be met at the national level. It will be a very long time before a comprehensive and accurate Dictionary of English Surnames can be compiled. There are, of course, numerous books on the subject, but some are perhaps too specialised to answer the general need and others, which adopt a more popular approach can be very inaccurate and misleading.

The modest aim of this booklet, therefore, is to provide accurate information about family names in the Bradford area and, if this proves successful, to deal in a similar way with other groups of Yorkshire surnames. The emphasis will be on names which originated in or near Bradford or which became important there in the period up to c1650. Some few distinctive names, which appear to have made Bradford their exclusive home after this date, will also be included, but there has been no attempt to cover the vast number of surnames which arrived in the area during the Industrial Revolution.

Bradford and district cannot be rigidly defined. The city's close neighbours include Keighley, Leeds, Dewsbury and Halifax and a recognition that each of these is also at the centre of a 'district', will help to define Bradford's sphere of influence. In fact this district goes beyond the confines of the ancient parish or manor, large though these were, and touches on areas which might be said to have dual allegiance. These include parts of the ancient parishes of Bingley, Calverley and Birstall, and one or two of the eastern townships of Halifax, notably in the neighbourhood of Northowram and Queensbury.

The surnames included here have of course been studied in the much wider national context, but even so there are several which cannot yet be satisfactorily explained. Some of the more obscure names e.g. Worsman, Suddards, Threapleton, Obank have been successfully identified, and some apparently straightforward names e.g. Ashton, Padgett, Pickles, Haworth are shown to have more complicated histories than is generally realised. The case of Ormondroyd highlights the particular difficulties arising from the use of an alias.

One advantage of studying these names as a group is the evidence they provide of the influence a single early migration can have on the distribution and ramification of a surname e.g. Tordoff, Lightowler, Silson. What also emerges in this respect is the significant role in earlier centuries of families such as the Tempests and territorial links in the estates of the great monasteries. Over all, however, Bradford's characteristic surnames testify to the influence of early migration from the north and west, with Halifax, Lancashire and the Yorkshire Dales predominant.

George Redmonds, 1990

Ackroyd, Akeroyd, Akroyd, Aykroyd

There is a locality known as Akroyd (i.e. oak tree-clearing) near Hebden Bridge. It is situated some 800ft above sea level, on the hillside to the east of Hebden water and looks across at Heptonstall. John de Aykroide, the constable for Wadsworth in 1381, seems to be the first of the name, but may be identical with the John, son of Richard taxed there two years earlier. For centuries the family lived in the same neighbourhood and there is a baptismal entry in the Heptonstall register which refers to Samuel Aykeroyd of Aykeroyd in 1648. Long before this date, however, Ackroyds had moved far afield and one family which settled in Lancashire adopted the unusual spelling Ecroyd. From a Bradford point of view the most significant aspect of this early expansion was the move into Haworth which was next to Wadsworth but in Bradford parish. Henry Akroyd had acquired interests there by 1478 and in two or three generations the surname was as prolific in Haworth as it was in Wadsworth. An Edward Aikrod was taxed 8 pence on lands he held in Bradford in 1545. The spelling 'Ackroyd' was a relatively late development but is now the conventional form of the name in Bradford, although both Akeroyd and Aykroyd are well established there. Akroyd is much more characteristic of the Halifax area.

1381 John de Aykroide (Wadsworth) WCR
1478 Henry Akroyd (Haworth) TN
1545 Henry Aikrod (Haworth) SR
1602 Henry Ackroyde (Haworth) PR

Aked

There is no reference to this surname in early Bradford records, including the detailed muster rolls and subsidy rolls of 1524-45, but as it is amongst the earliest entries in the parish registers, from 1596, it may have arrived in the parish soon after 1550. Certainly in 1641 the Akeds were well established in the town, and seem to have favoured baptismal names beginning with a 'J'. There is evidence that soon after this date one branch of the family moved into the neighbourhood of Shelf, part of Halifax parish, and further migrations took the surname eventually to Willow Hall and Kershaw House. By the end of the 18th century Aked was predominantly a Halifax name. The most likely explanation of Aked's origin, and one that is borne out by the varied spellings in Bradford in the period c1600, is that it derives from Akehead in Cumberland, but may have arrived in Bradford via Leeds, or a parish in the eastern half of Yorkshire. Certainly the surname was found in the 1540s in places such as Tadcaster and Cottingham.

1280 Richard de Aykeheved, SS 83
1379 John de Aykeheued (Thornton in Lonsdale) PTY
1558 Richard Aked (Tadcaster) WYR
1572 Agnes Ayckehead (Leeds) PR
1613-45 Tristram Aked/Akehead (Horton) PR

Akeroyd, Akroyd See **Ackroyd**

Aldersley

From Aldersley, a medieval settlement in Allerton. The family remained in the parish for at least 300 years, although the surname was never prolific. It seems likely that at least one branch moved into Airedale which is now the main home of the name. An identical surname in Almondbury probably became extinct in the 16th century.

1354 John de Aldoleghs (Bradford) CR
1488 William Alderleys (Bradford) WYR
1545 John Aldersles (Allerton) SR
1641 Peter Oldersley (Clayton) Prot R

3

Allerton

Allerton is a frequent place-name in Yorkshire and usually means 'the farmstead among the alder trees'. The surname had a number of independent origins and was recorded in the Yorkshire Pipe Rolls as early as 1191. Now, however, it is very uncommon, although a family with the name was prominent for centuries in the parish.

1230 Hugh de Hallerton (Bradford) EYCh
1415 John Allerton (Bradford) CR
1545 John Allerton (Allerton) SR
1641 Richard Allerton (Bradford) Prot R

Ambler

An 'ambler' in the Middle Ages was a horse with an easy-going disposition. Chaucer uses the word in this sense and it occurs in local wills well into the 1500s. In 1556, for example, Thomas Hardwick left 'on yong gray amblinge nagge' to his son in law. The surname Ambler seems likely, therefore, to have been a nickname, certainly in the Halifax area where much of its history can be traced. Other early examples of the surname in York, Farsley and Baildon may have independent origins, but there is some evidence to suggest a connection with the Halifax Amblers. For example the will of Richard Ambler, of Halifax, who died in 1526, makes it clear that he had interests in York, Farsley and Otley — a parish which then included Baildon. On the other hand the bequest to Richard Ambler of Ambler Thorn locates the family home in the area now called Queensbury, where several Amblers were taxed in 1545. It was in this area that the surname eventually ramified so successfully.

1307 Nicholas le Aumbleour WCR
1350 John Aumbelour (Warley) WCR
1489 Thomas Awmeler (Ovenden) YD
1545 John Aumler (Ovenden) SR

Appleyard

An account of the Appleyards in *The Yorkshire Genealogist* some years ago, discussed their origins in Norfolk and subsequent migrations through Lincolnshire into Yorkshire. This may be absolutely accurate but there is also clear evidence for the surname from the 13th century at least in villages as far apart as Thurlstone and Allerton near Bradford. This latter family may have been responsible for much of the surname's ramification in and around Bradford. In 1545, for example, there were Appleyards locally in Allerton (2), Horton and Clayton who seem likely to have been related and others at Hipperholme, Tong and Drighlington whose origins could lie elsewhere. Orchards were such a common feature of the medieval landscape that it would not be surprising if the surname had several origins. On the other hand it is not immediately clear whether it is simply geographical, indicating residence in a settlement near such an orchard, or whether it was partly occupational, denoting the dwelling-house of somebody with special responsibilities for the 'Appleyard' — possibly in the production of cider. In an interesting discussion on this subject Moorhouse (WYAS) identified the site of Allerton's 'Appleyard' which was known by 1664 as the Oaks, a name finally abandoned during development in the 1960s.

1351 William del Appelyard (Bradford) CR
1422 John Appillyerd (Allerton) CR
1545 Richard Appulyerd (Allerton) SR

Ashton

Because Ashton is a common English place-name it is tempting to think of it as the source of the local surname. However, there is no obvious Yorkshire place-name origin and although Eshton near Gargrave has the same meaning i.e. 'farmstead by the ash tree', and may have contributed to the surname's frequency, the probability is that Ashton locally is more often a variant of the Lancashire Aspden.

    1520 William Aspeden (Halifax), Clay
    1565-69 Ralph Aspeden/Ascheden/
            Ashton (Warley) PR
    1641 Laurence Ashden/Ashton
         (Hunsworth) PR

Atkinson

In the Middle Ages Adam was a popular Christian name in the West Riding and, through its diminutive Atkin, it gave rise to several quite independent surnames. Atkinson occurred consistently in Bradford records and may have had an origin there.

    1389 John son of Adam (Thornton) YD
    1421 Thomas Johnson Atkynson (Bradford) CR
    1539 Robert Atkynson (Manningham) MR
    1626 Silvester Atkinson (Bradford) WYD

Aykroyd See Ackroyd

Bailey

This surname and Bailiff are listed separately by Reaney but the evidence in Bradford suggests that they could have the same family origin. Various officials could be described as 'bailiff', for example a sheriff's deputy or a manorial steward, and the surname must have a number of independent origins. In the Bradford area it may have spread from Idle where it was hereditary by 1379.

    1379 Adam Ballef/Richard Bailif (Idle) PTY
    1423 John Bailly (Bradford) CR
    1528 Thomas Balie (Bradford) WYR
    1545 John Baily (Farsley) SR

Baines

A difficult surname. It was well established in and around Leeds in the early 1500s so the first Bradford families may have moved from there. Even earlier it was apparently hereditary in the neighbourhood of Ingleton, but it is recorded so widely, and so closely resembles other surnames, that it is impossible at this stage to be certain of its meaning. However, one possibility is that it was originally a nickname based on the Northern form of 'bones'.

    1219 Serlo Baynes (Yorkshire) Reaney
    1384 Robert Banes (Calverley) YD
    1526 John Banes (Tong) Tempest MSS/ 3/10
    1539 John Bayns (Manningham) MR

Bairstow, Barstow, Bastow

This common Bradford surname derives from the place-name Bairstow (i.e. berry-place), which once described an area of land straddling the ridge in Southowram, near Halifax. The surname is first recorded in the late 13th century at which time the family held land in both Hipperholme and Northowram. In the 1400s their main home appears to have been at Brown Hirst in Ovenden but as early as 1412 a branch had settled in Allerton and it was there and in Thornton that the surname ramified successfully. Bairstow was prone to variation from an early date and numerous alternative spellings developed as its area of distribution increased, including Baister, Basstoe, Bastey, Beastow and Beairstow. One particularly interesting development was in Shelf and Northowram, where the suffix 'stow' was for a long time replaced by 'stall', similar in both meaning and pronunciation, but inevitably suggesting confusion with Birstall.

    1284 Ralph de Bayrestowe (Hipperholme) WCR
    1350 Richard de Bairstawe (Halifax) WCR
    1420 John de Bayrstow (Shibden) YD
    1473 Robert Byrsthow (Allerton) WYR
    1539 John Burstow (Manningham) MR
    1564 Thomas Barstall (Shelf) PR

Balme, Baume

Balme is a variant spelling of Balne which, in the Middle Ages, was the name of a South Yorkshire township and also of a large area of land lying between the Aire and Don in their lower reaches. The place-name poses several problems to linguists but is generally taken to be descriptive of the wet lands which once characterised the region. Smith suggested that it came indirectly from Latin 'balneum' (i.e. bath). The family name had found its way into Bradford by the end of the 16th century and there are grounds for supposing this family had links with one at Temple Newsom. On the other hand Balmes were already settled in the adjoining parishes of Birstall and Halifax before that.

1292 Richard de Balne FY
1464 John Balne (Pontefract) WYR
1492-94 Brian Balne/Balme (Halifax) Clay
1541 John Bawme (Northowram) YD
1596 John Baume (Bradford) PR
1641 Thomas Balme (Bradford) Prot R

Balmforth, Balmford, Bamforth, Bamford

The place-names Bamford in Lancashire and Bamford in Derbyshire have the same meaning (i.e. footbridge by the ford) and both gave rise to surnames. The earliest Yorkshire references to the surname indicate migration from both these counties but a family settled in Halifax parish by the mid 1400s seems likely to have arrived there from the west. These Bamfords were tenants of the Saviles, a fact which seems to have influenced the dispersal of the name in West Yorkshire, and the first move into Bradford may have come via Wyke or Ovenden in the late 1500s. The development of 'forth' from 'ford' was a commonplace dialect pronunciation, but the spellings with a 'l' may have developed by analogy with the local surname Balme, or everyday words such as 'calm'. In any case Balmforth now outnumbers Bamforth in and around Bradford, although elsewhere in West Yorkshire this is not the case. In general the spelling Bamford seems likely to indicate a more recent migration from Lancashire.

c 1210 Thomas de Bamford (Fixby) EYCh
1456 Isabel Bawmeforth (Southowram) TN
1545 James Bawmfurth (Ovenden), Rober Balmfurth (Halifax) SR
1571 William Bawmeforthe (Wyke) CR
1641 John Balmforth (Bradford) Prot R

Banks

Bank is an extremely common element in minor place-names. The surname was no particularly common in the West Riding bu one prominent family held Bank Newto near Gargrave for several centuries an another ramified in Bradford.

1342 William de Banke (Bradford) CR
1422 John Bank (Bradford) CR
1524 John Banke (Bradford) SR
1641 Steven Bankes (Bradford) Prot R

Barracliffe, Barrowcliffe

Variants of Barraclough.
1506 John Beryclyfe (Bardsey) WYR

Barraclough, Barrowclough

There has been considerable speculatio about this prolific Bradford surname. Weekley said it derived from a locality near Clitheroe possibly having Barrowford in mind; Reane thought it probably came from near Wake field and Cottle just said it was from a 'los place in West Yorkshire'. In fact it was orig inally a Southowram surname, derived from a settlement now identified as having bee close to Barraclough Lane. A 'clough' wa a ravine and according to Smith the prefi was the Old English 'bearu', a grove or wood Although Barraclough was recorded in place such as Ripon and York in the 1400s most o the surname's history, from c1300 to c1500 was in Southowram and Hipperholme. How ever, a significant move saw Barraclough established in Birstall parish in the earl 1500s, at Wyke and Cleckheaton, and thi was the area in which the surname ramifie so spectacularly. By 1641 it was firmly est ablished in Wibsey and Bradford. Althoug Barraclough is now the conventional spellin in the Bradford area, the surname has many variants elsewhere and it is worth noting that in most cases these are very similar to spellings recorded in the Halifax area in the early history of the name. e.g. Barrowclough, Barrowcliffe, Berrycloth.

1315 Peter del Baricloughe (Hipperholme) WCR
1379 John Barowclofe (Southowram) HAS
1457 Peter Baroclogh (Southowram) YD
1524 William Barrowclogh (Southowram) SR
1545 John Baroclought (Wyke) SR

Barstow, Bastow See **Bairstow**

Bartle

Bartle has often been assumed to be a diminutive of Bartholomew but the Lancashire Bartles, who held land in Great Eccleston in 1334, almost certainly derived their name from the locality Bartle near by. The place-name has recently been explained as 'tongue of land on which barley grows'. There were also Bartles in that period holding land in Lower Ribblesdale, and they may have been the ancestors of a family settled in Bradford in the 1530s. The surname did not immediately flourish there but in more recent times it has become particularly prolific; so much so that Bartle is now predominantly a West Yorkshire surname.

1334 William de Bartaill (Wigglesworth) YF
1539 Percival Bertyll (Bowling) MR
1641 James Bartles (Bradford) Prot R
1689 Joshua Bartle (Bradford) WYD

Bates

The Christian name Bartholomew was not very common in the West Riding in the 13th and 14th centuries, but it gave rise to a number of surnames through its pet-forms and diminutives. These included Bate and Batt, Baty and Batty and they appear to have been interchangeable to a certain extent. This may also be true of the surnames

derived from them, especially in the first generations. As a result the early history of a surname like Bates is particularly complicated. There was, for example, a hereditary surname Bate in the Thornes area of Wakefield which acquired a final 's' before 1500 and which seems likely to be connected with the Bates families at Ovenden and Sowerby in the same manor. The surname ramified successfully in that area and by 1545 was also present in Idle. Not surprisingly, perhaps, it had become relatively common in Bradford by 1641.

1332 Ralph Bate of Thornes and Thomas his son. WCR
1349 Henry, son of Thomas Bate (Thornes) WCR
1379 Henry Bate (Wakefield) PTY
1491 Robert Bates (Southowram) YD
1545 Robert Baites (Sowerby) SR

Baume See **Balme**

Bentley

The place-name Bentley (i.e. bent-grass clearing), is common in the West Riding and gave rise to several family names which are in no way connected. One of these localities was in Shelf, close to the boundary with Hipperholme, where the surname Bentley has a long and well-documented history. Although a Clayton family recorded in the 14th century seems likely to have the same origin, this is not necessarily the case, for a second place-name quite different in origin (i.e. Bencliff) also gave rise to a surname which could easily have been absorbed by Bentley.

1349 Henry de Bentelay (Hipperholme) WCR
1494 Henry Bentley (Shelf) YD
1545 Arthur Bentley (Shelf) SR
1295 Adam de Bennetlive (Bradford) BAS
1342 Robert Bencliff (Bradford) BAS

1379 Robert de Bentelay (Clayton)
PTY
1414 John Bentley (Heaton) CR

Berrycloth
A variant of Barraclough.
1572 Richard Barowclouthe (Halifax)
PR

Binns
Binns was said by one writer to derive
from the Old English personal name
Bynni, and elsewhere it has been
explained either as 'a maker of binns'
or 'a dweller in the hollows'. Even if
such explanations are valid for the surname in other parts of the country they
ignore completely the present distribution of Binns in the West Riding and its
history in the Bradford area. That distribution is the result of the surname's
ramification in the last 450 years for
in 1545 most of the Yorkshire families
with the name lived in Haworth or
Allerton and it is there that the records
confirm a place-name origin, probably
the hamlet now known as High Binns,
in Oxenhope. There are several minor
places with the same name and they
were derived by Smith from an Old
English word meaning a manger or stall.
1346 Jordan del Bynnes (Oxenhope)
WPB
1478 Laurence Binns (Haworth) TN
1545 Richard Byns (Haworth) SR

Birkby
From Birkby, a locality in Thorner.
The early spellings show that the first
element is 'bretta', meaning 'of the
Britons'.
1277 Robert de Bertby WCR
1379 William Bretteby (North
Bierley) PTY
1480 John Birtby (Northowram)
WCR
1545 William Birkby (North Bierley)
SR
1641 John Birkby (Bradford) Prot R

Birkenshaw, Birkinshaw
Derived from Birkenshaw, a locality in
Birstall parish. There are over twenty
variants of the surname in all, some of
them particularly common in other
parts of Yorkshire. This may be partly
the result of early migrations, which
took the surname to Leeds, Wakefield,
Barnsley and York, but there were also
Birkenshaws in Lancashire from at least
1277, and this surname may have its
origin in a Lancashire place-name. The
Yorkshire surname is recorded as early
as 1274 and by the end of Henry VIII's
reign was numerous in the townships
to the west of Bradford. The muster
roll of 1539 included families at Clayton, Manningham, Horton and Thornton. By 1641, however, it had ceased
to be important there.
1288 John de Birkynschaye (Birkenshaw) YD
1447 John Byrkynshaghe (Birkenshaw) WB
1524 Gilbert Byrkynshay (Calverley)
SR

Blackburn
This common Yorkshire surname usually derives from Blackburn in Lancashire, but in Bradford, where it arrived
comparatively late, it must often be a
variant of Blackbrook. (See Blagborough)
1596 Marmaduke Blagburne (Bradford) PR
1600 William Blakburne alias Blake-
brooke (Waddington) WYR
1609-16 Walter Blagbrooke/Blage-
burne (Bradford) WYD
1641 Francis Blagbara/Blackborne
(Bradford) PR; Prot R

Blagborough, Blagboro, Blagbrough, Blagbro, Blakeborough, Blakebrough
Variants of Blackbrook. Reaney derived
the names from localities in either
Devon or Norfolk, but their distribution

and history point to a Yorkshire origin in the area south-west of Skipton. It is there that Blackbrook is first recorded as a surname and that the development into 'Blackbrough' can be seen to take place. A move to Bowling in c1600 by one family accounts for the frequency of the surname in and around Bradford, and the same variation in the suffix occurred there. The place-name Blackbrook (i.e. black stream) is first recorded in Barnoldswick parish in the 12th century. See also Blackburn.

- 1379 Henry Blakbrowk (Carleton in Craven) PTY
- 1522 Robert Blakebroghe (Broughton) LB
- 1578 Thomas Blakbrouke (Gisburn) WYR
- 1590 Arthur Blaikebroughe (Gisburn) WYR
- 1600-09 Walter Blakebrooke/Blagbrooke (Bradford) WYD; PR
- 1641 Francis Blagbara (Bradford) PR

Blamire, Blamires, Blaymire, Blaymires

The surname probably means 'dark, swampy place', as Reaney suggested, but there is no evidence that it has a Yorkshire origin despite his suggestion that it might derive from 'Blamires' in the West Riding. Neither the place-name nor the surname occurs in early Yorkshire records and his own evidence concerned a family living in Cumberland in 1250. This seems much more likely to be where the surname originated. In the 16th century, however, Blamire(s) occurs first in the North Riding and then in the Wibsey area, where the family were tenants of the Rookes of Royds Hall. It is numerous now in West Yorkshire particularly in and around Cleckheaton.

- 1527 William Blamyre (Boltby) YF
- 1598 John Blaymires (Wibsey) WYD
- 1673-77 Joshua Bleamers/Blaymire/Blamire (Oakenshaw) PR

Boland, Bolland, Bowland

The place-name from which these names derive is Bowland and it refers both to a township in Lancashire and a forest area associated with it, much of which is in Yorkshire. The 'bow' is thought to refer to a significant bend in the River Ribble. The surname occurred in Sawley Abbey charters in the 13th century, but is first recorded in Bradford in the 1500s. Significantly, perhaps, John Bolland was a member of Dame Rosamund Tempest's household in 1539.

- 1467-68 William Bolland (Calverley) YD
- 1522 Robert Boland (Bolton by Bowland) LB
- 1545 Robert Bolland (Bradford) SR
- 1641 John Bolland (Wyke) Prot R

Bolling, Bowling

As a township in Bradford parish Bowling was formerly divided into Great or West Bowling and Little or East Bowling and the wide hollow between the former and the Park was judged by Smith to be the 'bowl' of the place-name. A surname 'de Bolling' is recorded as early as 1166 in the Yorkshire Pipe Rolls and this man may be the ancestor of the family who later held the manor and had Bolling Hall as their seat. The Bollings owned land in many parts of Bradford by the end of the 14th century and soon became one of the foremost West Riding families. After Bolling Hall passed to the Tempests in 1497, as a result of Rosamund Bolling's marriage to Richard Tempest, the father moved to an estate in Heaton and the line was continued through his son Edward. One descendant later settled in Virginia, about the time of the Restoration, and the surname is still known in the United States. Here it survives as Bowling, but Bolling appears to have disappeared completely.

1379 John de Bollyng (Bowling)
PTY
1488 Robert Bolling (Bowling)
WYR
1543 Edward Bollinge (Bradford)
WYR
1641 Edward Bolling (Bradford)
Prot R

Booth

An exceptionally prolific surname with several independent West Riding origins. The place-name from which the surnames derive is Scandinavian in origin and means a 'temporary shelter'; some of those eventually became permanent settlement sites. Booth was also used to describe the subdivisions of the forest vaccaries in both Lancashire and Yorkshire. In the Bradford area there seem to have been two quite distinct sources of the surname. Boothtown in Northowram was originally 'Booths', in the plural, and the surname in this case retained the final 's' for a very long period. In Shipley, however, there was a Booth family where the place-name origin is not readily identifiable.

a)1298 Richard del Bothes (Sowerby)
WCR
1379 John de Bothes (Northowram)
PTY
1483 John Bothis (Halifax) Clay
1545 Edward Boithes (Northowram)
SR
1609 Daniel Boothes of Boothestowne, WYD

b)1346 Hugh del Bothe (Bradford) CR
1379 Roger del Bothe (Shipley)
PTY
1467-68 William Both (Shipley) YD
1545 William Boith (Shipley) SR

Bottomley

Bottomley was the 'clearing in the valley bottom' and originally referred to a sub-division of Barkisland, sufficiently important to be described occasionally as a township. There is still a fine old house at the heart of the settlement. The surname, which has a history of at least 700 years in that part of Yorkshire, very soon found its way into neighbouring parishes and there were Bottomleys in the Colne and Holme valleys from 1434. By 1545 it was also established in Northowram and this is possibly where the first Bradford families came from. It is now both prolific and widely distributed.

1277 Henry de Bothemley (Scammonden) WCR
1379 John de Bodhomlay (Barkisland) PTY
1471 William Bothomlaye (Barkisland) WCR
1545 Roland Bothomley (Northowram) SR
1641 Hugh Bothomley (Bradford)
Prot R

Bower

There is evidence to show that more than one Yorkshire family inherited the surname Bower and, in the case of a family at Handsworth (Sheffield), it is clear that the 'bower' was an important dwelling house. This probably explains the origin of the Bradford surname which had its early history in Bowling but soon spread to Allerton and Horton. By 1641 it was one of the commonest surnames in the parish.

1342-46 Cecilia Bogher/Bower (Bradford) CR
1415 Thomas Bower (Bradford) CR
1524 Thomas Bower (Bradford) SR
1572 Thomas Bower (Bradford) WYD

Bowland See **Bolland**

Bowling See **Bolling**

Bradford, Bradforth

The place-name, which means simply the 'broad-ford', is common generally and occurs twice in Yorkshire, so clearly the surname could have multiple family origins. The surname certainly occurred in Bradford but it did not remain there long so it may well be connected with families established in Dewsbury, Wakefield and Lower Wharfedale in the 16th century. For example the will of John Bradford of Warmfield (1495) shows that he had interests in property at Boldshay, Wilsden and Clayton.

1291 John de Bradeforthe (Pudsey) YD
1331 Geoffrey de Bradeford/Bradforth (Wakefield) WCR
1379 John de Bradeford (Soothill) PTY
1411 Thomas Bradforde (Thornton) CR
1459 William Bradford (Horton) Th 2

Brigg, Briggs

A prolific surname with multiple origins; the north country form of 'bridge'. The final 's', which is not found in the early history of the name, is now usual and Brigg is largely confined to Airedale. There was some confusion between Briggs and Brighouse.

1342 Thomas del Bryg (Bradford) CR
1422 Adam Bryg (Bradford) CR
1545 John Brige (Haworth) SR
1674 John Briggs/Brighouse (Kirkburton) QS

Brook

This surname has far fewer origins than is usually said to be the case and in West Yorkshire there appear to be two main sources. The more important numerically was probably the Huddersfield family but Brook also ramified in and around Birstall parish, where it may have had an independent origin, and this is a more likely source for the single Brook taxed in Bradford in 1545.

1379 John Bethebroke (Liversedge) PTY
1467 Thomas Bythebroke (Clifton) WCR
1524 Richard Brooke (Cleckheaton) SR
1561 William Broke (East Bierley) YD

Brooksbank, Brookbank, Brockbank

The main ramification of Brooksbank has been in and around Bradford. The surname was certainly established in the Thornton/Clayton area by 1545 and in Allerton perhaps as early as the 1370s. Although its origin could therefore be local the family probably moved into Bradford from Warley, just over the hills in Halifax, for the Brooksbanks were prominent there for centuries. The meaning of the surname is straightforward, and there have been few variants but the precise settlement site has not been identified and the 'brook' in question could lie in either parish.

1371 Thomas Bythebrokebank (Warley) WCR
1379 Thomas Brokesbank (Warley) PTY
1379 John Brokesbaule [sic] (Allerton) PTY
1545 John Brokysbank (Thornton) SR

Burnley

This is almost exclusively a Yorkshire surname now and it has a history in the West Riding from the early 14th century. It is tempting therefore to link it with Burn Lee, a locality near Holmfirth, but the early spellings of the place-name make this most unlikely, e.g. 'le Brendeley' or 'burnt clearing' (1308) WCR. The more likely source is Burnley in Lancashire (i.e. clearing by the river Brun), for in this case the spellings of the place-name and surname show a parallel development. There was, moreover, a good deal of movement from Burnley into Yorkshire, e.g. John Pakmon of Brunneley (1317) WCR, who may have been a pedlar. Much of the surname's early history was in Lower Wharfedale, close to Ilkley, and other Burnleys were living in Birstall from the 14th century. However, Thomas Burnley of Eccleshill (1545) was said to be the son of a Skircoat clothier, and appears also to

11

have had interests at Longroyd Bridge in the Colne Valley. These three places, some distance apart, were all in the manor of Wakefield, where tenants called Burnley are recorded through the 1400s.

1305 William de Brunleye (Ilkley) YF
1379 Richard de Brunlay (North Bierley) PTY
1416 John Brunlay (Yeadon) CR
1521 Thomas Burnelay (Longroyd Bridge) WB

Busfield

Probably from Bousfield in Westmorland originally, but it may have arrived in Airedale via York.

1567 Jacob Bowsefell (York) FY
1581 John Busfeld (York) FY
1613 James Busfeilde (Leeds) PR
1617 Wilfrid Bosfield (Calverley) PR

Butterfield

There is no obvious West Riding locality from which Butterfield could have derived, although 'Boterfeld myre' (1343) in Easington pre-dates the first references to the surname. It may be, therefore, that the source is in Lancashire where Simon de Butterfield is recorded c1250. By 1379, however, the family was well established in Bowland with branches in Newton, Mitton and Slaidburn, and this in itself suggests that they had been in that district for some time. Although the surname remained in Bowland it was widely distributed in Yorkshire by 1600 with a major concentration in Keighley, Bingley and Bradford.

1379 Adam de Butterfeld (Newton in Bowland) PTY
c1485 Edmund Butterfeld (Bolton by Bowland) YAS
1510 John Butterfield (Keighley) MR
1535 Edward Butterfield (Bradford) BAS

Cawthra, Cawthraw, Cawthray

Few surnames have changed their appearance as dramatically as Cawthra, for it has evolved via Cawdray and Corderoy from Querderay. In modern French this is 'coeur de roi' meaning 'heart of a king', and probably a nickname in origin. Much of its history was in Lower Wharfedale, first at Ilkley and later at Bramhope, but by the end of the 16th century the name had arrived in Pudsey. Cawthra is essentially a Bradford surname but a dozen similar variants are found in other parts of Yorkshire.

1290 John Quir de ray (Ilkley) YD
1402 Adam Cawdray (Burley) Th 6
1524 Robert Cawdrey (Otley) SR
1592 Thomas Cawdrey (Pudsey) YF
1641 Samuel Cautheray (Pudsey) Prot R

Chellow

This was 'Ceol's-hill' (Smith), the name of a Heaton settlement first recorded in Domesday Book. The surname from it, which now appears to be extinct, had only a short history in Bradford but survived elsewhere in Yorkshire into the late 16th century.

1338 Cicilia de Chellowe (Bradford) CR
1379 John de Chellowe (Heaton) PTY
1458 John Chellowe (York) FY
1573 Thomas Chelley (Escrick) WYR

Chippendale, Chippindale

Almost certainly from Chippingdale in Lancashire (i.e. market-place valley). The surname occurred there from the late 13th century but had arrived in Wyke by 1379. There it was sometimes confused with Shibden, the local place-name. Its ramification was late.

1379 Richard Chipyndale (Wyke) PTY
1431 William Schippingdale alias Schipden WCR

1545 Edward Chippyndaill (North
Bierley) SR
1641 Jonas Shipindale (Bradford)
Prot R

Clarkson

It could mean 'son of the clerk' or
'son of a man named Clark'. In either
case it had a number of independent
origins and was particularly well
established in the Wakefield area
c1524.

1359 Robert Clerkson (Haworth) CR
1545 Robert Clerkson (Bradford) SR
1641 William Clarkson (Bradford)
Prot R

Clayton

The Claytons locally took their surname from the Bradford township of
Clayton (i.e. farmstead on clay), and
they were considerable landholders
there as early as the 12th century.
However, the place-name occurs elsewhere, both in the West Riding and in
other parts of Northern England, and
the surname certainly has more than
one origin. In fact much of the ramification can be traced to the Claytons
of Clayton West.

c 1200 Adam de Clayton (Clayton)
KM
1330 Adam de Clayton (Clayton)
YD
1463 John Clayton (Bowling) WYD
1545Robert Claiton (Liversedge) SR

Clough

'Clough', meaning a ravine is a common
element in minor place-names but the
surname seems unlikely to have had
many Yorkshire origins. Its present-
day frequency in Bradford must owe a
great deal to a family recorded in Bowland from the 13th century which later
ramified in the Keighley area. However,
Cloughs in Northowram may have
belonged to a different family.

1332 William del Clogh (Thornes)
WCR

1379 William de Clowe (Wyke) PTY
1508 Simon Clogh (Hipperholme)
Clay
1545 Robert Clought (Northowram)
SR

Cockcroft, Cockroft

From a locality in Rishworth: the prefix 'cock' could be interpreted as the
domestic cock, the woodcock, or
possibly even a haycock. Much of the
surname's early ramification was in
Keighley, Ovenden and Wadsworth,
from where it doubtless soon moved
into Allerton.

1297 John de Cockecroft (Sowerby)
WCR
1488 John Cokcroft (Keighley) YD
1530 Henry Cokcroft (Holdsworth)
YD
1545 John Cokcroft (Ovenden) SR
1641 John Cockcroft (Allerton)
Prot R

Collinson

'Son of Colin', a diminutive of Nicholas
via the pet form 'Col'. The name had
several Yorkshire origins and is found
in Bradford in the 14th century.
Unfortunately it has not yet proved
possible to establish a link between this
family and the one established later in
Horton.

1354 Richard Colynson (Bradford)
CR
1519 Robert Colynson (Elland) Clay
1539 Adam Colyngson (Horton) MR

Cordingley, Cordley

Although Cordingley is one of Bradford's most characteristic surnames,
and was first recorded in Bowling
nearly 700 years ago, its origin and
early history are complicated. Part of
the problem is that the surname
appears to have had two alternative
forms, Cordingley regularly interchang-
ing with Cordley. In fact the element
requiring explanation is likely to be
'Cordon' rather than 'Cording'.

Although the first references clearly point to a place-name origin, this has not yet been identified. It seems unwise to presume that it must have been in Bowling for the surname also occurred in the 14th and 15th centuries at Allerton Gledhow near Leeds. The one important link between Allerton and Bowling is that Kirkstall Abbey possessed property in both. Whatever the origin it was in Bowling that the surname finally prospered, although much of its expansion took place in those parts of Birstall parish which were close to Bowling. For example there were generations of Cordingleys at Toftshaw and East Bierley.

- 1295 Robert de Cordelay (Bradford) BAS
- 1349 Robert de Cordenlay (Bowling) CR
- 1524 John Cordyngley (Bowling) SR
- 1589 Nicholas Cordyngley or Cordley (Birstall) Leeds PR

Crabtree

Derived from a lost settlement meaning 'crab-apple tree'. This may have been near Sowerby, but a locality named 'Crabtre' is referred to in Bradford court rolls (1355). The surname was well established in the Thornton area by c1540 and was among the dozen commonest surnames in Bradford a hundred years later.

- 1391 John de Crabtre (Sowerby) WCR
- 1472 John Crabtre (Stansfield) WCR
- 1539 Richard Crabtree (Allerton) MR

Craven

At the time of the Domesday survey Craven was the name of a vast region which included villages as far to the west as Hornby and Melling in Lancashire. More recently it has been used to describe a region covering parts of Airedale, Wharfedale and Ribblesdale. Its meaning is obscure, but it is thought to be Celtic in origin and may be connected with the word for garlic. As a surname it was in use over 800 years ago and later occurred in all three Ridings in circumstances which make it appear most unlikely that those bearing the surname were related. It is not just that Craven served as a surname for those who had left the district, for several families named Craven lived in Craven in the Middle Ages and it was a common name there in the early 1500s. In 1522 there were Cravens listed in Stainforth, Giggleswick, East Marton, Appletreewick, Carleton and Thornton in Craven. Despite that, Bradford is now at the centre of its distribution, and it seems likely that much of this ramification stems from one or two families. For example the only Craven in the Bradford muster of 1539 was Robert Craven of Heaton, but by 1641 it was a common surname in the town.

- 1384 William de Craven (Oakenshaw) YD
- 1411 Thomas de Craven (Bradford) CR
- 1519 Thomas Craven (Northowram) Clay
- 1545 Widow of John Craven (Northowram) SR
- 1569 Robert Craven (Bradford) CR

Croft

Although 'croft' has retained its original meaning of 'a small enclosure', it also gave rise to several early settlement names and these in turn gave rise to surnames. The first Bradford families called Croft probably came from Tong or other parts of Birstall parish.

- 1524 Thomas Croft (West Ardsley) SR
- c1530 John Croft (Birstall) YD
- 1545 John Croft (Tong) SR
- 1641 Thomas Croft (Bradford) Prot R

14

Crosley, Crossley

From Crossley (i.e. cross-clearing), a locality in Allerton. The main ramification of Crossley was in the Rochdale/Todmorden area and this seems likely to derive from Cross Lee. However the Thornton family of Bradford held land in Rochdale in the 13th century so it is possible the two are connected.

1190-1220 William de Crosselay (Allerton) EYCh
1379 John Crosselay (Allerton) PTY
1412 John Crosselay (Bradford) CR
1545 Richard Crosley (Bradford) SR

Darnbrook, Darnbrough, Darnborough, Downbrough, Downsborough, Downsbrough

From Darnbrook (i.e. hidden brook), a secluded hamlet on Malham Moor. It was held by Fountains Abbey and initially the Darnbrook family were tenants there. Subsequently they moved to other abbey properties at Bewerley and Rainton, but from the 1530s the surname became more widely dispersed, occurring first in Ripon and York, but reaching the Bradford area in the 1600s. It was there that the local pronunciation of 'down' produced new variants. c.f. Blagborough.

1361 William de Dernbrok (Darnbrook) YAS 140
1476 Thomas Darnbroke (Bewerley) WYR
1546 William Darnebroke (Bewerley) WYR
1635 Roger Darnebrough (Birstall) PR
1641 John Danbrooke (Bradford) Prot R
1666 Robert Darnborough (Tong) HT

Dawson

'Son of Daw', which is usually explained as a pet form of David. One problem with this is that Dawson is both frequent and widely distributed in Yorkshire in the 14th century, at a time when David was not in common use. It may be, therefore, that Daw was a pet form of some other Christian name, possibly of Ralph or even Rolf, on the analogy of Robert/Dob and Roger/Dodge. Dawson is prolific in Bradford, but has no obvious origin there. It was, however, well established in the Pudsey and Headingley areas in the early 1500s.

1524 John Dawson (Pudsey) SR
1539 Robert Dawson (Bradford) MR

Dean

Dean is from 'denu', the Old English word for 'valley' and a common element in local place-names. Despite this frequency it is unlikely that the surname has many origins in West Yorkshire and most of the early references are to families in Halifax. By 1545 there were two major concentrations of the surname, one at Horsforth and the other in and around Warley.

1297 Richard del Dene (Sowerby) WCR
1379 Richard del Den (Warley) PTY
1412 John de Dene (Sowerbyshire) Bradford CR
1524 Robert Deyn (Warley) SR
1539 Miles Dean (Clayton) MR

Denby

A common Bradford surname. It derives from the place-name Denby (i.e. the Danes' village), but as there are several Denbys in Yorkshire the problem is to identify which is the most likely source. The obvious choice seems to be Denby in Allerton, but there is some doubt as to whether or not this was an early settlement site. It was recently suggested that it was, on the grounds that a Sveinn de Denby held the moiety of an assart in Allerton in the 12th century. This is far from convincing evidence and may actually point to the Denby in Upper Whitley as the more likely source. A family named Denby were prominent tenants in Upper Whitley in the 12th and 13th centuries, no doubt taking their name from the settlement which then had township status. It was a Henry, the son of Sveinn de Denby in Upper Whitley, who finally sold all but three acres of his land there to the monks of Byland Abbey, helping them to become the principal landholders in the vill and accelerating its depopulation and loss of status. The surname Denby then disappeared from Upper Whitley and turned up in Allerton, where, incidentally, Byland Abbey also had land. The family is recorded in a variety of 14th century Bradford documents and one Thomas Denby was referred to in 1411 as 'the farmer of the town of Bradford', a clear indication of the family's status. As the first recorded reference to the locality Denby in Allerton calls it 'Denby Haull' (1521), it is probable that this particular place was named after the family. [See also Ledgard, Northrop, Liley]

1175-86 Osbert de Denebi (Denby) YD
c 1247 John de Deneby (Denby) YD
1379 John Denby (Allerton) PTY
1546 John Denbte (Haworth) YD

Denham, Denholm, Denholme

Probably from Denholme near Thornton (i.e. the valley water-meadow). Ther earliest surname references are clearly derived from this place-name, but there is as yet little evidence of continuity between these and the families recorded two hundred years later. In fact the name is missing from all the major Bradford documents between 1379-1545. One possible explanation for this is that the family

had an alias during that period or used an abbreviated form of their name, (c.f. Ormondroyd). Alternatively the source might lie outside the county. From the 16th century Denham has been principally established in the Hartshead/Hipperholme area.

1339 Robert de Deneholme, senior (Oxenhope) YD
1579 Thomas Denham (Bradford) WYR
1613 Thomas Denholme (Bradford) PR ___ ___ ___

1573 William Deynhum (Lightcliffe), Halifax PR
1592 William Broadley, alias Deanhome (Birstall) PR
1640-42 George Denham/Denholme (Hartshead) PR

Denison, Dennison

'Son of Denis', a popular saints' name, often written Dionis in the 13th and 14th centuries. The surname had a small number of origins in the West Riding, but none apparently in Bradford. A family in Yeadon may have been responsible for the expansion in Bradford and Leeds, although there were other Denisons in Birstall.

1524 Alexsander Denyson (Yeadon) SR
1574 Robert Dynnyson (Yeadon) WYR
1641 Samuel Dineson (Pudsey) Prot R

Dickinson

'Son of Dicon', a diminutive of Richard via the pet form Dick. It had several West Riding origins, including one in Midgley (Halifax) and one in Bingley.

1379 John Diconson (Bingley) PTY
1539 Richard Dykynson (Bowling) MR
1545 Edward Dicconson (Bradford) SR

Dickson, Dixon

'Son of Dick', a pet form of Richard, and one of Bradford's commonest surnames in 1641. It was a name with several different origins in West Yorkshire but in the period 1539-1545 there was a significant group in Haworth and Allerton. Dixon is the more common spelling now.

1342 Thomas Dicson (Bradford) CR
1422 Thomas Dicson (Bradford) CR
1539 William Dykson (Haworth) MR
1641 Jarvase Dixon (Bradford) Prot R

Dobson

'Son of Dob', a pet form of Robert and a name with several West Riding origins. It is prolific in Bradford, and in 1545 was recorded in Hipperholme, Wyke, Bingley, Shipley and Sowerby.

1298 John, son of Dobbe de Overam, WCR
1379 John Dobson (Sowerby) PTY
1412 John Dobson (Bradford) CR
1539 John Dobson (Thornton) MR

Dracup, Draycope

A difficult surname with an obscure but apparently unique origin. Yorkshire records appear to contain no reference to Dracup before c1580, after which time its migration from Ripley to Otley and Calverley can be roughly traced. It arrived in the neighbourhood of Idle in the 1600s but it was much later, in the Great Horton district of Bradford, that its major expansion took place. If Dracup has a place-name origin it could be explained as 'dragon valley' but as yet there is no evidence that this is the case. It is worth noting moreover that the Dracups were Catholics at a time when persecution obliged some families to adopt an alias. Such aliases were not necessarily very different in appearance, e.g. Hipperson for Hipperon; Hopperton for Hopton, so Dracup could have been a form of Draket, the name of another recusant family at Hampsthwaite not far from Ripley. This is, however, pure speculation in the face of a total lack of early evidence.

1583 George Drakopp (Ripley) PR
1625 John Drakeup (Otley) PR
1627 John Drackupp (Calverley) PR
1685-1709 Mary Dracupp/Draycup (Leeds) PR

Drake

The meanings suggested by Reaney include 'draca', the Old English word for a dragon and the less dramatic 'male of the duck'. It is prolific now in Bradford and appears to have had a single local origin in Shibden (Northowram).

1275-1298 William Drake (Shibden) WCR
1379 John Drac (Northowram) PTY
1456 John Drake (Shibden) YD
1524 John Drayk (Northowram) SR
1539 William Drake (Thornton) MR

Driver

Usually considered to be an old form of 'drover', but descriptions such as 'clothedryver' (1555) and 'wolledriver' (1606) suggest that it may have been a local word for a carrier. The early history of the surname is obscure, with isolated references occurring over a relatively wide area. There is some evidence to suggest that a family was based in the Otley area but the main ramification took place after 1600 in the townships to the north-west of Bradford, notably in Haworth.

1379 John Dryuer (Skipton) PTY
1420 John Dryver (Bradford) CR
1474 Richard Dryver (Rishworth) WCR
1535 Thomas Dryver (Lindley) MR
1545 John Dryver (Hawksworth) SR
1626 John Driver (Thornton) YD

Dufton

From a locality in Westmorland (i.e. either the farmstead with doves or the farmstead of a man name Dove). There are a few scattered references to the surname in Wharfedale (1276), York (1341) and Ripon (1503), but it was in Leeds and then in Pudsey that it eventually ramified.

1584 Alice Dufton (Leeds) PR
1641 William Dufton (Pudsey) Prot R

Eastburn, Eastbourne

From the locality near Steeton in Kildwick parish (i.e. east-stream). The surname is first recorded c1200 and by the end of the 14th century it was relatively numerous, with families in Steeton, Glusburn, Sutton and Thornton in Craven. By 1545 there were also Eastburns in Haworth and Bradford, but Kildwick continued to be the surname's main home for some time. It is rare there now, but well established in Hull where it might be thought to derive from Eastburn in the East Riding. Curiously there is no early evidence for such a derivation and the Hull Eastburns seem likely to have originated in Airedale.

1379 Laurence de Estburn (Steeton) PTY
1473 Thomas Estburn (Eastburn) YAS 132
1539-45 Omfray Estburn/Estborn (Bradford) MR; SR
1550 Thomas Estborne (Kildwick) PR

Edmondson, Edmundson, Emonson

'Son of Edmond', a very common name now in Bradford but with no obvious local origin. There was a numerous family of this name in Barnoldswick in the 1500s.

1473 John Edmondson (Storiths) YAS 132
1522 Richard Edmondson (Barnoldswick) LB

1543 Alan Edmondson, John Edmundson, George Emundson (Barnoldswick) SR

Ellingworth, Ellingford, Ellinsworth

Rare variants of Illingworth.

1379 John de Elyngworth (Bowling) PTY
1545-76 Nicholas Hillyngworth/ Yellingworthe (Haworth) SR; WYR
1684 William Ellenforth (Kildwick) PR
1766 Thomas Illingworth otherwise Ellingworth (Wilsden) QS

Ellis

From 'Elis', the Middle English form of Elias. It probably has more than one origin locally, but a Bradford family has been largely responsible for its expansion.

1379 John Elys (Bradford) PTY
1423 Thomas Elys (Bradford) CR
1524 Edward Ellys (Bradford) SR
1539 John Ellys (Bradford) MR

Ellison

'Son of Elis', i.e. Elias. It has several Yorkshire origins e.g. 1350-79 John, son of Elias the clerk; Robert, son of John, son of Elias the clerk; Robert Elisson (Thurgoland) YD, PTY. Ellison was numerous in Craven by 1522 and this area seems likely as the source of the Bradford family.

1379 John Elysson (Horton in Ribblesdale) PTY
1456 Henry Elyson (Littondale) SS 130
1522 Laurence Ellyson (Keighley) LB
1537 Laurence Ellison/Elyson (Horton) WYD

Elsmore, Ellsmore (?)

These rare surnames may be surviving variants of the very unusual surname

Elysmagh. See Watmough.
1379 John Elysmagh and wife
'Johannes filius Elysmaghe'
(Newsholme in Bowland) PTY
1545 Thomas Ellesmoge (Swillington)
SR
1556 Robert Ellismouth(Swillington)
PR
1633 Edward Ellsmith (Sheffield) PR

The surname arrived in Bradford in the early 17th century.
1617-42 Miles Ellesmore/Elsmugge
(Bradford) PR

Elsworth, Ellsworth
From Elsworth (i.e. Elli's enclosure), a lost settlement in Fewston parish. The surname is now common in Bradford having arrived there via Calverley and Tyersall.
1361 William de Ellesworth (Dacre)
SS 42
1527 Robert Ellesworth (Hampsthwaite) SS 104
1609 John Elsworth (Calverley) PR

Emmott
From Emmott in Lancashire (i.e. junction of streams). The family lived in the Colne area and is referred to frequently in Lancashire documents from the 13th century. However the real expansion took place in the West Riding and it was prominent in Haworth and Airedale from c1540.
1296 Henry de Emmott (Emmott)
VHL
1443 William Emmott(Emmott) VHL
1539 Laurence Emmot (Haworth)
MR

Emsley, Hemsley
Common now in Bradford where it arrived relatively late. In earlier centuries it was widely distributed, occurring in major centres such as Hull, York and Ripon, as well as in smaller villages such as Carnaby and Drax.

From the earliest evidence it is clear that more than one family had the surname and that it could be derived from either Helmsley near Pickering or Gate Helmsley. These are both North Riding place-names but they have quite different origins and the spellings reflect this difference.
1301 John de Helmesley (Nawton)
SR
1303 William de Hemelsay (York)
FY
1379 John de Helmeslay (Ripon)
PTY
1481 George Elmyslay (Ripon) SS64
1539 Bartholomew Elmysley
(Halton) YAS 132

Exley
Probably from Exley in Southowram, although there is another Exley in Keighley. The meaning is the same in either case, i.e. 'church clearing'. The fascination in these place-names lies in the combination of the British element 'eclesia' with an Anglian suffix, suggesting that the locality may be the site of an early British church. The surname now is prolific and widely distributed in the western half of Yorkshire, but the ramification was late, only one Exley being recorded in the 1545 subsidy roll for the Halifax area. The family had early links with Bradford but much of the expansion probably took place in the Rawden area where Samuel Exley settled c1650.
1274 William de Ecclesley WCR
1379 John Eglessay (Southowram)
PTY
1412 John Eccleselay (Bradford) CR
1488 Thomas Ecclesley (Haworth)
YD
1641 Samuel Exley (Bradford) Prot R

Farnish
A rare variant of Furness.

1716 George Farnish/Furnies (Mirfield) PR
1754 Isaac Farnis otherwise Furnis
(Kirkheaton) QS

Farrand, Ferrand, Ferrant

Probably a nickname from Old French
'ferrant' i.e. iron grey. The family held
land in Skipton and Carleton in Craven
from c1300 and the surname was in
Bradford by the 1500s.
1306 Hugh Ferraunt (Skipton) YI
1522 Robert Ferrant/Farrant (Skipton) LB
1524 John Ferand (Bingley) SR
1539-45 Thomas Ferrand/Farrand
(Clayton) MR; SR
1641 George Farrand (Bradford)
Prot R

Fawcett

From Fawcett in Westmorland (i.e.
multi-coloured hill-side). The surname
ramified in and around Sedbergh where
it occurred as early as the 13th century.
By 1545, for example, there were no
fewer than fourteen Fawcetts taxed
there. It reached Leeds in the 1500s
and Bradford soon afterwards and is
now prolific in both places.
1321 Thomas de Faghside (Sedbergh)
YD
1428 Adam de Faxsyde (Sedbergh)
YD
1504 William Fawsett (Leeds) WYR
1641 Thomas Fawcet (Bradford)
Prot R

Fawthorp, Fawthrop

Fawthrop has an unusual origin and
its history begins with the Favel or
Fauvel family. They owed their name
to an Old French word meaning
'tawny' or 'fallow-coloured', and are
recorded in Yorkshire in the 12th
century holding land in Broughton
near Skipton. Their property was
probably named after them and title
deeds refer both to Richard Fauvel

and Richard de Fauvelthorpe c1300.
Unfortunately 'Fauvelthorpe' cannot
now be identified, but the surname
prospered in the Skipton area and was
eventually modified to Falthorpe and
Fawthorpe. In the 1400s it became
established in Giggleswick and at a
later date found its way to York and
Halifax. Its history in Bradford dates
from the early 1500s.
1303-43 Richard de Fauvelthorpe
(Broughton) YD
1379 Richard de Famelthorpe [sic]
(Broughton) PTY
1454 John Falthorp (Giggleswick)
WYR
1536 Robert Falthorpe (Bradford)
BAS

Fearnley

From one or more place-names in
Yorkshire (i.e. fern(y)-clearing). These
include Farnley near Leeds, Farnley in
Wharfedale and Farnley Tyas. As the
surname was particularly common in
Birstall parish, from the 1300s at least,
the source there may be High Fernley
in Wyke.
1358 Thomas del Fernylegh (Wyke)
CR
1379 John Fernelee (Wyke) PTY
1450 Catherine Fernlee (Bradford)
BAS
1545 William Fernley (East Bierley)
SR

Fearnside, Fearnsides

Probably from Fernside (i.e. fern-
slope), a small locality near Colne in
Lancashire. The surname occurs there
from the 13th century in hamlets close
to the border with Yorkshire, where
the first examples date from c1330.
One family settled in Ribblesdale, and
as the surname prospered there it is
uncertain whether the first Bradford
families came directly from Lancashire
or via Bowland. For example an entry
in Bingley parish register for 1598

records the burial of Edmond Fearnside 'a traveller of Gisburne'. Certainly there were Fearnsides before that in Ovenden and Bradford and by 1641 the name was numerous. It was in the 17th century that the final 's' became more commonplace.

1296 Peter del Fernyside (Trawden) VHL
1503 John Fernssyd (Rimington) YAS 56
1539 Thomas Fernnysyd (Bradford) MR

Feather

In the 16th century Feather is recorded as far south as Woolley and Darton; in the Leeds area at Kippax and Rothwell and in several Airedale localities. A family in Bingley, tenants of Rievaulx Abbey's grange at Faweather, seems to have been responsible for the expansion in Airedale and Bradford which now characterises the surname. Before 1500, however, Feather's history is obscure. Reaney has suggested that it is metonymic for 'feathermonger', or perhaps a nickname, but it might also be an abbreviated form of Featherstone.

1385 Thomas Fether (York) FY
1391 Robert Fether (Bowling) YD
1522 Richard Fedder (Glusburn) LB
1539 George Feder (Bradford) MR

Ferrand, Ferrant See Farrand

Field

When surnames were becoming hereditary the 'field' was the open arable field of the community and it gave rise to a number of minor settlement names in Yorkshire. It is likely therefore that the surname had several different origins, including one in Bradford. [See also Fieldhouse.]

1346 William del Feld (Bradford) YD
1414 Thomas de Feld (Bradford) CR
1524 William Feyld (Horton) SR

Fieldhouse

A common Bradford surname which may derive from a locality in the Bowling area. After c1400, however, it is absent from Bradford records for a very long period, so its present frequency may be the result of late immigration. Alternatively Field and Fieldhouse may have been aliases in much the same way as Hammond and Ormondroyd.

1342 John de Feldehouse (Bradford) BAS
1356 John del Feld (Bowling) CR
1391 John del Feldhouse (Fieldhouse in Bowling) YD

Firth

Although 'firth' seems to have been a general word for woodland in Old English it came to refer more specifically to an area of forest or free chase in West Yorkshire. In Elland, for example, there were frequent references to the escape of beasts in 'Le Frith' and this may have referred to a stretch of woodland in Rishworth and Norland. The surname Firth, which derives from this word, is prolific in Yorkshire and has more than one family origin, but a major expansion in the Elland area stemmed from Firths in Rastrick and Barkisland who may have shared a common origin. The two hamlets of Firth House, one in each township, seem to mark the families' homes but it may also be that the sites were in some way connected with the supervision of the 'Frith'. By the early 1500s the surname had spread beyond Elland, although it was still very common there, and there were Firths in most neighbouring parishes, including Bradford.

1275 Walter del Fritht (Rastrick) WCR
1379 John del Firth (Rastrick) PTY
1416 Thomas de Fyrth de Rastryke WCR

1416 Thomas de Fyrth de Bothomley
   WCR
1539 John Firthe (Bowling) MR

Flather, Flathers, Flatters

This surname is unusual enough to
suggest a single family origin. It has a
long history in the neighbourhood of
Leeds, particularly in Pudsey, and
there are early references in Bradford.
Nevertheless it poses several problems,
for there is nothing obvious to link the
Pudsey family with Flathers recorded
as far away as Normanton (1338);
Goldthorpe (1456) and York (1530);
nor is the meaning clear, and the one
Pudsey spelling which suggests that it
may have been occupational, i.e.
'flayer' or skinner, was probably a mis-
reading.

1379 Roger Flayer [sic] (Pudsey)
   PTY
1411 William Flethyr (Allerton in
   Bradford) CR
1475 Richard Flather (Pudsey) CR
1539 Richard Fladder (Bolton in
   Bradford) MR
1540-45 Richard Flatter/Flaider
   (Hartshead) YAS 80; SR

Fletcher

From the Old French word for an
arrow-maker. It is a common surname
and had several Yorkshire origins.
There is no doubt, however, that it has
often absorbed the surname Flesher,
also occupational, but derived from
'flesh hewer', an Old English word for
butcher. By c1540 there were Fletchers
in Idle, Horton and Eccleshill but it
would be difficult to separate their
origins.

1379 John Fleshewer, carnifex
   (Rothwell) PTY
1379 Robert Flecher (Hipperholme)
   PTY
1412 Nicholas Fleschewer (Bradford)
   CR
1539 William Flecher (Horton) MR
1545-46 William Fletcher/Flesher
   (Otley) SR

Foster

A common and widely distributed sur-
name with numerous Yorkshire origins.
The evidence suggests that in the
Bradford area it was usually 'forester'.

1274 Robert the Forester WCR
1379 Thomas Forester (Liversedge)
   PTY
1539 William Foster (Allerton) MR
1545-46 Anthony Foster/Forster
   (Bingley) SR

Furness, Furniss See Farnish

From Furness, a district name referring
to the northern, detached part of
Lancashire which was separated from
the rest of the county by Morecambe
Bay. The surname is recorded in Yorkshire from the 12th century and was
firmly established in Mirfield and
Birstall by the 14th. From there it
appears to have spread to both Halifax
and Bradford.

1313 Alan de Furneys WCR
1379 Richard de Fournays (Mirfield)
   PTY
1471 Ralph Forness (Halifax) WYR
1488 Richard Fournes (Haworth) YD
1539 John Fournes (Horton) MR

Gant

An alternative form of Gaunt.
1142 Robert de Gant. YAS 25, 30
1545-67 Thomas Gawnt/Gante
   (Dewsbury) SR; WYR

Garnett

A surname known in York and South
Yorkshire from the 14th century and
very common now in Bradford. However the Bradford Garnetts seem likely
to have arrived, via Bowland, from
Lancashire, where the name is first
recorded in the 12th century. According to McKinley they survived there as
landowners without ramifying as
successfully as many other Lancashire
families. A certain Benedict Gernet,
who was chief forester for Lancashire

in the reign of Richard I, is referred to in early Bowland documents.

1510 John Garnett (Bolton by Bowland) MR
1522 Richard Garnet (Skipton) LB
1539 Edward Garnet (Bradford) MR

Gaunt

Probably from Ghent in Flanders. The surname has a very long history in Leeds and is common now in the Bradford area. There were families in Dewsbury and Pudsey (1545), and Wyke (1585).

1199 Maurice de Gaunt (Leeds) Th 45
1379 Peter de Gaunte (Thornhill) PTY
1545 Richard Gaunt (Pudsey) SR
1566 Alexander Gawnte (Wibsey) WYD

Gibson

'Son of Gib', a pet form of Gilbert. The early Bradford examples of the surname do not necessarily point to an origin in the parish for there were Gibsons close by at Pudsey and Northowram.

1379 Thomas filius Gilberti (Horton) PTY
1412 Thomas Gybson (Bradford) CR
1459 Thomas Gibson (Pudsey) Th 2
1539 James Gybson (Bradford) MR

Gledhill

From Gledhill (i.e. kite hill), named when the kite was a common bird of prey in the West Riding. The settlement site has not been identified, but was almost certainly in either Stainland or Barkisland, where the family was living in 1275. The Gledhills continued to be prominent in the Elland/Sowerby area but by 1550 the surname had spread south to the Colne Valley, east to Thornhill and north into Allerton. Other Gledhills settled in parts of South Yorkshire e.g. Conisbrough (1506) and West Bretton (1542).

c 1290 Henry de Gledehyl (Stainland) YD
1379 Thos de Gledhill (Stainland) PTY
1523 John Gledehill (Stainland) YD
1539 Robert Gledhill (Allerton) MR

Goldsborough, Goldsbrough, Gouldsborough, Gouldsbrough

There are two distinct Yorkshire surnames, one from a locality in the North Riding parish of Lythe and the other from Goldsborough near Knaresborough. The two have different meanings but the West Riding locality is 'Godel's fortification'.

The family taking its name from this village were important landowners in the Knaresborough area from c1150, and there was still a Goldsborough at Goldsborough Hall in 1540. However, by this time other Goldsboroughs had settled in the villages of Tong and Thornton, both close to Bradford, where the surname eventually expanded. The possible connection here is through the Thornton family who, like the Goldsboroughs, were tenants of Kirkstall Abbey.

1379 Richard de Goldesburgh, chivaler (Goldsborough) PTY
1471 Edward Goldisburgh (Goldsborough) YD
c 1525 Thomas Goldsburgh (Tong) Tempest
1539 William Golburghe (Thornton) MR
1641 Thomas Gouldsbrough (Bradford) Prot R

Goodall

Probably 'good ale', a nickname for a seller of good ale (c.f. 1301 William Sourale SR). In south Yorkshire the surname might be from the place-name Gowdall but in the Calder Valley it occurred over long periods in Horbury and Birstall and by c1540 was well established in Bradford and villages to the south and east. It was

23

confused at times with Gooder/
Goodheir/Goodyear.
- 1309 Robert Godale (Horbury) WCR
- 1460 Thomas Gudeale (Birstall)
  WYR
- 1480 William Godeale (Horbury)
  WCR
- 1539 James Goodale (Bradford) MR
- 1565 John Goodale alias Goodare
  (Rastrick) WCR

Gouldsborough, Gouldsbrough
See **Goldsborough**

Green
Said to derive from residence near the
village green, but in fact the 'greens' in
the Bradford area were often patches
of common grazing well away from
the village centre and there are West
Riding examples of families with
Green as a surname living in isolated
hamlets called Green House. Although
the surname has multiple origins it is
still distinctive enough locally for the
early history of some families to be
traced. For example a Green family
genealogy has been worked out for the
period 1286-1600 demonstrating a
migration from Newsholme in Bowland
to Horsforth, and pointing to a link
with Greens who were millwrights in
Frizinghall in the 17th century.
- 1286 Adam de la Grene (Newsholme)
  MD 335
- 1369 Edmund del Grene (Newsholme) MD 335
- 1481 John Gren (Horsforth) MD 335
- 1573 Gabriel Greene (Horsforth)
  MD 335

Greenall, Greenald
Variants of Greenhough.
- 1600-04 John Grenall/Grenehall/
  Greneald (Eccleshill) PR

Greengate
A common Yorkshire place-name denoting a 'green road' or a settlement site

alongside it. The surname is recorded
from 1277 and one family had a long
history in Allerton. It appears now to
be extinct.
- 1379 Thomas de Grenegate (Allerton)
  PTY
- 1524 William Greyngaytt (Allerton)
  SR
- 1641 Robert Greengate (Wilsden)
  Prot R

Greenhough, Greenough
A common Bradford name, said by
Reaney to be from place-names such
as Greenhow. However the evidence
locally establishes that it is usually a
variant of the Lancashire surname
Greenhalgh which arrived in west
Yorkshire in the 1400s and was later
associated with Eccleshill and Idle.
[See also Greenald.]
- 1461 Henry Greneall (Hipperholme)
  WCR
- 1545 Edward Grenall (Eccleshill) SR
- 1559-64 Cuthbert Greneall/Gren-
  houghe (Halifax) PR
- 1614 John Grenehall/Grenehaughe
  (Bradford) PR

Greenwood
From Greenwood in Heptonstall. This
spectacularly prolific surname ramified
initially in the Calder valley and in
1545 no fewer than 23 Greenwoods
were taxed in Halifax parish. Much of
the expansion into Bradford took place
via Haworth, where 13 Greenwoods
were listed in 1641 compared with one
in Bradford.
- 1275 John del Grenwode (Sowerby)
  WCR
- 1430 Thomas Grenewod (High
  Greenwood) WCR
- 1524 John Greynwod (Allerton) SR

Grimshaw
From Grimshaw in Lancashire, a place-
name usually said to mean a wood
where there was a spectre or goblin.

The surname was known in Lancashire in the 13th century and in Northowram from the early 1500s.

1519 William Grymshay (Northowram) Clay
1545 Edward Grymsthey [sic]
   (Northowram) SR
1584 Richard Grymshaye (Northowram) PR

Grimwood

A variant of Greenwood, possible influenced by Grimshaw.

1519 John Grynwod/Grymwoode
   (Halifax) Clay

Hainsworth

From Hainworth, a small locality near Keighley, possibly meaning 'thorn bush enclosure'. Alternatively the first element could be the Old English personal name 'Hagena'. The medial 's' in Hainsworth is a comparatively late development resulting from the dialect speakers' problems with the possessive 's', but also owing something perhaps to confusion with the Lancashire surname Ainsworth. The two surnames have quite different origins, and Hainsworth is first referred to in an early 13th century Airedale charter. As early as 1298, however, a William de Hagenewrth married a Hipperholme woman, to become a tenant of land there, and by the poll tax of 1379 the family was settled in Allerton. Actually the transcript of this document has inadvertently delayed recognition of the migration into Bradford, for the surname appears there as Haueworth, possibly because the writer was linking it with Haworth not far away. It was in Allerton and the neighbouring villages that Hainsworth ramified and in the various rolls of 1524-45 there were branches of the family in Wilsden, Thornton, Clayton and Manningham. Remarkably, although Hainsworth is now very common, it is this area which is still at the heart of its distribution.

1273 Walter de Hannewrthe
   (Bingley) YI
1379 John Haueworth [sic]
   (Allerton) PTY
1494 John Haynworth (Allerton)
   YD

Haley

A very common Bradford surname which had its origins in Hipperholme in the 13th century. Although it clearly derives from a place-name, the exact source is not certain for Haley Hill in Northowram appears to be named after the family and Hayley in Oxenhope is not well documented. It may be that the locality was in Hipperholme but that the site was abandoned c1350. From the early spellings the meaning is 'enclosure clearing'. The surname quickly established itself in Ovenden, just to the north west of Hipperholme, and first occurred in Bradford records in 1327. By the early 1500s there were Haleys in Thornton, and a Richard Haley acquired interests in Little Horton in 1526. The spellings of this period suggest that there may even then have been confusion with similar surnames such as Healey.

1277 John de Haley (Hipperholme)
   WCR
1379 Roger de Heyle (Hipperholme)
   PTY
1379 John de Hala (Ovenden) PTY
1483 John Halay (Ovenden) YD
1545-52 Abraham Hailey/Halay
   (Bradford) SR; WYR

Hall

Probably for a person working at 'the hall'. It has multiple origins, one apparently in the Bowling/Horton area.

1343 Roger del Halle (Bradford)
   CR
1379 William del Hall (Bowling)
   PTY

1488 Richard Hall (Horton) YD
1545 Thomas Hall (Horton) SR

Halliday

Possibly a name given to a child born on a 'holy day'. It has no obvious local origin but is recorded before c1540 in Ripon, York and several other parts of Yorkshire. There were Hallidays in Birstall and Halifax from about that time and eventually the name ramified in Baildon/Shipley where it is still very common.

1545 Richard Haliday (Ovenden) SR
1587 Roger Holliday (Idle) PR
1641 Richard Halliday (Bradford) Prot R

Halmonroyd, Holmonroyd

These rare variants of Ormondroyd survive in Leeds. They are actually closer to the original form of the name, but developed an 'l', probably by analogy with words such as 'half'.

1626 John Almanroid (Bradford) PR

Hammond See Ormondroyd

Hanson

'Son of Han', a pet form of Henry. Locally the name originated in Rastrick and by c1540 was common there and in Quarmby. Although these two townships were some miles apart, both were in the same administrative division of Wakefield manor. Hanson eventually established itself in the Allerton/Haworth area.

1545 John Hanson (Rastrick) SR
1566 John Hanson (Wibsey, witness to deed) WYD
1592 John Hansonn alias Mortymer (Thornton) WYR
1641 Edward Hanson (Bradford) Prot R

Hardacre, Hardaker

A prolific Bradford surname now. It originated in Ribblesdale and appears

to derive from an unidentified place-name there. It was established for several centuries in Hellifield and Long Preston in particular but expanded into Airedale before 1600.

1304 Alexander, the forester of Hardaker (Gargrave) YI
1379 Nicholas Harthacre (Hellifield) PTY
1510 John Hardaker (Hellifield) MR
1543 Thomas Hardacre (Hellifield) SR
1588 Michael Hardacre (Kildwick) PR

Hardy

Originally a nickname from the Middle English 'hardi' (i.e. bold or courageous). It has multiple origins in Yorkshire and is first recorded there in the 12th century. The earliest Bradford references occur in the 1500s, but where they came from is uncertain.

1524 Richard Hardy (Wadsworth) SR
1539 Richard Harde (Bolton, Bradford) MR
1574 Robert Hardye (North Bierley) WYD
1615 William Hardie (Thornton) YD

Hargrave

A form of Hargreaves.

1524 Thomas Hargrave (Hunslet) SR
1545 William Hargraves (Hunslet) SR
1666 Peter Hargrave (Tong) HT

Hargreaves

An exceptionally prolific surname, which appears to have originated in Lancashire in the 13th century. It is discussed by McKinley who notes a place-name near Whalley as the likely source. The first Yorkshire references, in the 14th century, occur close to the border with Lancashire at that point and support McKinley's conclusion. The name ramified quickly and by c1540 it was common in Calderdale and well established in the Leeds area.

Tong, where one Hargreaves family settled at an early date, was linked manorially with Cowling on the Lancashire border, and in this case the migration may have been direct.

1502 Lawrence Hargreaves (Halifax) Clay
1526 George Hardegraves, (Cowling) Tempest
1539 Henry Hargraves (Bradford) MR

Hartley

Although this name is exceptionally prolific in Bradford there are significant numbers elsewhere, both in Yorkshire and Lancashire, and the surname may have several origins. McKinley commented on a source in Rochdale parish and there are at least two other possibilities in the West Riding. The Westmorland place-name Hartley seems a less likely source on the face of it, but its early spellings (i.e. Harkeley, Herclay) parallel those of a family settled on the Yorkshire/Lancashire border in the 13th and 14th centuries. This complicated origin should not obscure the fact that Hartley has a 600 year history in Bradford, having ramified initially in the Haworth area. It would not be surprising if this family, like so many others, had moved there from Upper Calderdale.

1308 John de Hertlay (Stansfield) WCR
1379 Adam de Hertlay (Haworth) PTY
1415 John Hertlay (Haworth) CR
1539 John Hertley (Manningham) MR

Haste

A variant of Hayhirst, which probably had a Lancashire origin. It developed in the late 17th century.

1615-24 Richard Harst/Hast/Hairs (Calverley) PR
1684-95 Theodore Hayhirst/Hayrst/ Haste (Bradford) PR

Haworth

One or two early references to Haworth as a surname clearly derive from the place-name Haworth, a township in Bradford parish, but there is no evidence to link these with the 16th century Haworths. In most cases these can be shown to be variants of other surnames, their spelling influenced no doubt by the place-name.

1548-62 John Hayward/Hayworth/ Haward/Haworth (Kirkburton) PR
1540-43 Robert yanyn alias Hayvyerd (Dewsbury) PR
1540-43 Robert Ganinge aliter Haworthe (Dewsbury) PR
1603 William Haworthe als Hayward (Saddleworth) YF
1725-35 Charles Haworth/Howarth/ Howard (Sheffield) PR
1763-65 John Hayworth/Haworth/ Howarth (Kirkheaton) WB

Heaton

Locally from Heaton (i.e. high-farmstead), a township in Bradford parish. It was sometimes called Heaton in Bradford Dale to distinguish it from other West Riding Heatons e.g. Kirkheaton, Cleckheaton. The surname had more than one origin but the Bradford family eventually ramified in Haworth.

1335 Adam de Heton (Bradford) CR
1415 William Heton (Bradford) CR
1545 Wilfrid Heton (Haworth) SR
1641 Robert Heaton (Haworth) Prot R

Hellas, Heelis, Heeles

These could be alternative forms of Hillas, or even Ellis.

1522 John Elys (Skipton) LB
1543 John Helys, Richard Heles (Skipton) SR
1608 Christopher Helehouse (Leeds) PR
1641 Richard Heeles (Addingham) PR

27

Hemingway

From a minor locality in either Hipperholme or Southowram which cannot now be identified. The Scandinavian personal name Hemingr was still in use c1300 and the meaning of the place-name was probably 'Hemingr's way'. The surname is evidenced from the 14th century, ramified initially in Southowram and soon spread to Birstall and Dewsbury.

- 1309 Richard de Hemmyngway (Hipperholme) WCR
- 1379 William Hemyngway (Southowram) PTY
- 1474 John Hemmyngway (Southowram) YD
- 1545 Richard Hemyngwey (Northowram) SR
- 1641 Robert Hemingway (Bradford) Prot R

Hemsley See Emsley

Hey

Hey (i.e. enclosure) is a very common minor place-name in the West Riding but the surname's origin is in Barkisland. Much of its early ramification took place in Quarmby (Huddersfield) but in the 17th century it was also common in Bradford.

- 1569 William Heye (Bradford) CR
- 1600 Robert Hey (Bradford) WYR
- 1641 Thomas Hey (Bradford) Prot R

Hill

The name is prolific in Bradford and much of its expansion took place in Allerton. There are, however, numerous other Hill families elsewhere in the British Isles.

- 1342 Thomas of the Hill (Bradford) BAS
- 1415 John del Hill (Allerton) CR
- 1545 James Hill (Allerton) SR
- 1641 Luke Hill (Allerton) Prot R
- 1678 James Hill, a Scotchman (Bradford) PR

Hillas

From the surname Hillhouse, first found in Tong and Calverley. On the face of it a derivation from a locality such as 'Hillhouses' (Smith) seems likely, but no early references have been found. It may therefore have an origin outside Yorkshire or even be a variant of a better known surname. [See Hellas.]

- 1513 Gilbert Hylhouse (Birstall) WYR
- 1545 Gilbert Hilhous (Bowling) SR

Hindle

From Hindle (i.e. hind-hill), a locality in Whalley, Lancashire. There has been some confusion with Hindley, and both names are found in Bowland and Airedale before reaching Bradford. Hindle is numerous now in Bradford.

- 1543 John Hyndle (Glusburn) SR
- 1577-80 Richard Hindell/Isabel Hindley (Mitton) WYR
- 1641 John Hindle (Bradford) Prot R

Hobson

'Son of Hob', a pet form of Robert. In the 16th century it was particularly numerous in the vicinity of Hawksworth where members of the Baildon family used it as an alias.

- 1545 William Hobson (Hawksworth) SR
- 1557 William Hobson otherwise Baildon (Hawksworth) CR
- 1600 Thomas Hobson otherwise Baildon (Hawksworth) CR
- 1607 John Baildon alias Hoobson (Horsforth) WYR

Hoddy See Oddy

Hodgson

'Son of Hodge', a pet form of Roger. It has several origins but the local family was prominent in Bowling and may descend from an important Horton merchant. It was one of Bradford's commonest surnames by 1641.

1345 Thomas son of Roger (Horton) CR
1379 Thomas filius Rogeri, merchant (Horton) PTY
1463 Thomas Hogeson (Bowling) WYD
1545 James Hogson (Bowling) SR

Holdsworth

From Holdsworth (i.e. Halda's enclosure), a locality in Ovenden. The surname is recorded from c1200 and it was already numerous by 1545 with many families settled in and around Northowram. At the same time there were already Holdsworths in Bradford, Clayton, Allerton and Bowling, and it has been a prolific surname in the town ever since. A south Yorkshire hamlet with the same name also gave rise to a surname.

1275 John de Haldewrth WCR
1379 John Haldeworth (Ovenden) PTY
1460 John Haldeworth (Hipperholme) YD
1524 John Haldisworth (Northowram) SR

Holgate, Howgate

The place-name means 'hollow way' and occurs several times in Yorkshire. There are two such localities in Calderdale, where the surname is recorded from the 13th century and may have two origins. It is likely that the first Bradford Holgates came from one of these sources, but not certain, for the surname occurs elsewhere in the North.

1274 Thomas de Holgate WCR
1379 Magota Holgate (Warley) PTY
1459 Thomas Holgate (Halifax) WYR
1565-70 John Holgate/Houlgate/Howgate (Northowram) PR

Hollindrake, Hollingdrake, Hollingrake, Hollinrake

The source of these surnames is an unidentified minor locality near Todmorden, and the family lived in Stansfield for over a century. The term 'rake' was applied to a rough path and 'hollins' were stands of holly bushes. (See Hollings). In the 1400s, or so the evidence suggests, the family moved into the Wilsden/Bingley area, and the name is still well established in Haworth.

1275 Adam del Holirakes WCR
1376 John de Holinrake (Stansfield) WCR
1489 John Holynrak (Allerton) Will BAS
1533 Thomas Holyngrake (Wilsden) WYR
1630 Thomas Hollingdrake (Bingley) WYR

Hollings, Hollins, Holling, Hollin

The hollin or holly tree was used as winter fodder for cattle in the Pennines and Hollins is one of the commonest minor place-names in the West Riding. Despite that the surname does not appear to have numerous origins and much of the significant Yorkshire ramification can be traced to families in Clayton and Rawdon.

1310 William del Holyns (Rawdon) YD
1361 Roger del Holyns (Clayton) CR
1411 Robert de Holyns (Bradford) CR
1524 Thomas Holyns (Clayton) SR
1545 Constantine Hollyngs (Rawdon) SR

Holmes

Prolific in Yorkshire, with multiple origins. Much of the ramification in Bradford can be traced to a family in Oxenhope and Haworth: Holme (i.e. water meadow) occurs there as a minor place-name. This family name had a final 's' from the 14th century, whereas in general the change from Holme to Holmes took place in the late 1500s. A

Halifax family, which may have influenced the expansion of the surname in Bradford, probably originated in Sedbergh, with Holme near Kendal a possible source in this case. The surname may also have absorbed the Slaithwaite Hawme.

1339 Adam del Holme (Oxenhope) YD
1379 Robert de Holmes (Haworth) PTY
1508 Robert Holmys (Oxenhope) WYR
1545 Christopher Holms (Haworth) SR

Holmonroyd See **Halmonroyd**

Hopkinson

'Son of Hobkin', a diminutive of Robert, based on the pet form Hob. It originated in Sowerby, spread to the Allerton area by c1540 and later ramified in Haworth.

1374 John Hobkynson (Sowerby) WCR
1415 John Hobkynson (Sowerby) WCR
1524 William Hopkynson (Sowerby) SR
1545 William Hopkynson (Allerton) SR

Horsfall

A prolific Yorkshire surname derived from Horsfall, (i.e. horse-clearing), a locality near Todmorden. Much of the family's early history was in Heptonstall chapelry but there were significant moves to Huddersfield and Birstall in the 1400s, and over the ridge into Haworth in the early 1500s. [See Horsfield.]

1316 William del Horsfal (Calder Valley) WCR
1379 Richard del Horesfall (Stansfield) PTY
1481 Thomas Horsfall (Halifax) Clay

1524 William Horsfall (Haworth) SR
1641 Samuel Horsfall (Haworth) Prot R

Horsfield

A common variant of Horsfall. There is a natural tendency in colloquial speech to follow a final 'l' with 't' or 'd' e.g. Bramall, Bramald and in the case of Horsfall this was reinforced because it made the surname meaningful.

1784 Richard Horsefield otherwise Horsfall (Halifax) QS

Horton

A common English place-name. The surname has several origins but locally, where it is first recorded in the 12th century, it is from Great or Little Horton (i.e. farmstead on dirty land).

1246 Swain de Horton (Thornton) YI
1342 Thomas de Horton (Bradford) BAS
1421 John Horton (Bradford) CR
1539 Nicholas Horton (Horton) MR
1641 Tristram Horton (Bradford) Prot R

Howgate See **Holgate**

Hoyle

Prolific in the West Riding where it probably had several origins. It is a dialect form of 'Hole', a common minor place-name. One of the biggest ramifications was in Halifax parish, but the surname also expanded in Scammonden and Slaithwaite. One possible source, therefore, is 'Hole' in Sowerby.

1297 Ivo del Hole (Sowerby) WCR
1379 John Hole (Sowerby) PTY
1524 John Hoyle (Sowerby) SR
1545 John Hoill (Idle) SR

Hudson

'Son of Hud', a pet form of Hugh. It

was frequent and well distributed in the West Riding in the 14th century. Although there is no evidence of a Bradford origin the name was well established in Baildon and Bingley in the 16th century.

1545 Stephen Hudson (Baildon) SR

Hustler

Probably a northern form of 'ostler', the keeper of a hostelry. The evidence in the West Riding points to a single family origin in Silsden, but from there the surname soon spread to Bradford where it is still well established.

1379 Robert Husteler (Silsden) PTY
1522 William Husteler (Silsden) LB
1539 Thomas Hustler (Manningham) MR
1641 Thomas Hustler (Bradford) Prot R

Ickringill, Ickeringill

This very distinctive surname derives from a locality in Beamsley. It is Scandinavian in origin and means 'squirrel ravine'. By the early 16th century the family was living in Kildwick parish, first at Silsden and then at Cowling. Although one branch moved soon afterwards into Lower Wharfedale, it is likely that the first Haworth family moved directly from Kildwick or Keighley.

1379 John Icornegill (Beamsley) PTY
1522 Thomas Ynkcornegill (Silsden) LB
1579 Henry Hickorngill (Cowling) WYR
1641 William Ickorngill (Haworth) Prot R

Idle

Reaney has shown that Idle could have several different origins, but there is no doubt that locally it derives from the township of Idle, formerly part of Calverley parish. The meaning of the place-name has caused much speculation but both Smith and Ekwall suggest that it originally described 'idle' or uncultivated land. The surname has never been numerous locally, but is recorded consistently from the 12th century.

c 1190 Ailsi de Idle (Calverley) Th 6
c 1270 Elias de Idell (Calverley) Th 6
1397 John de Idle (Pudsey) YD
1459 John Idle (Pudsey) Th 2
1545 William Idill (Manningham) SR

Illingworth, Illingsworth

See also **Ellingworth**

Exceptionally prolific in Bradford. It derives from the locality Illingworth (i.e. Illa's enclosure), which was formerly part of Ovenden and continued to be the family's home for centuries. However, as early as the 14th century the surname had settled in Bowling and its expansion in Bradford parish in the years before 1545 was remarkable. In the subsidy roll of that year there were Illingworths at Bolton, Manningham, Allerton, Heaton, Haworth, Bowling and Bradford: further afield, but still in the Bradford area, were the Illingworths of Baildon and Calverley.

1277 Adam de Hyllingworth WCR
1361 Matthew de Illyngworth (Bradford) CR
1450 William Yllingworth (Bradford) BAS
1524 John Illyngworth (Allerton) SR

Ingham

Particularly prolific in Bradford and Halifax. Its history there goes back to the early 1400s when Thomas de Ingham of Lincolnshire was granted land in Southowram. The apparently strong links between Halifax and Lincolnshire at that time seem to have affected the dispersal of a number of surnames (see Waterhouse). Clearly the Lincolnshire village of Ingham (i.e. Inga's dwelling-place) is the most likely source in this case, but the place-name occurs in other English counties and there may also have been confusion with Hingham.

1379 Richard Hyngham (Ecclesfield) PTY
1424 Thomas de Ingham (South-owram) YD
1516 Laurence Yngham (Halifax) YD
1545 Laurence Yngham (Bradford) SR

Jackson

Although Jackson is now prolific in all parts of Yorkshire and was widespread even in the 14th century there is no clear evidence for a Bradford origin. There were Jacksons living in Clayton, Thornton and Bradford in 1539, but their connections with one another, or with other Jackson families, have not been established.

1344 John Jackson (Bradford) CR
1539 Hew Jakson (Thornton) MR

Jerrison

A rare variant of Margerison. It developed when the stress was placed on the second syllable. In his will of 1758 John Margerison of Tong made Robert Gerison a trustee, but the variant is evidenced a century earlier in Adel parish register.

1676 John Jerrison (North Bierley) QS

Jowett, Jowitt

From 'Juetta', a diminutive of Juliana based on the shortened form 'Jull' or 'Juwe'. The personal name was popular from c1200 and there was a Jowett Barton in York as late as 1438. Many of the earlier spellings suggest that its pronunciation formerly rhymed with 'duet' and this is still how it is said in North America where a Bradford family

settled in the 17th century. Although the name had more than one origin the majority of Jowetts seem likely to share a common ancestry in Bradford. Between 1500 and 1640 it ramified so successfully that no fewer than 65 Jowetts were listed there in 1641. No other local name could match this, although several came close to it in the Haworth area.

e.g. 1343 Thomas, son of Juliana (Bradford) CR
1346 Adam Jowet (Bradford) CR
1495 John Jowett (Clayton) BAS
1539 Leonard Jooet (Clayton) MR
1586 William Jewet (Thornton) WYR

Judson

'Son of Jud', a pet form of Jordan. It is said that the Crusaders brought back water from the river Jordan for the baptism of their children and certainly Jordan was popular as a baptismal name in the West Riding in the 13th century. The surname appears to have had an origin in Stanbury, but the evidence is not yet conclusive.

1340 Jurdan de Stanbury. CR
1343 Roger Juddeson (Stanbury) CR
1415 John Judson (Stanbury) CR
1625 John Judson (Stanbury) CR

Kellett

The surname has a long history in Yorkshire. In the 13th and 14th centuries it occurred occasionally in the North Riding and York, but it was in Bradford that the major expansion took place. It derives from one of several place-names in the North-West, all having the same meaning (i.e. spring-slope) and the most likely sources are the North Lancashire villages of Over and Nether Kellet.

1472 Richard Kelett (Hartshead) WCR
1539 Thomas Kellet (Allerton) MR
1600 Robert Kellitt (Bradford) PR

32

Kent

Probably from the county of Kent rather than from the river Kent. The surname occurs frequently in Yorkshire records from the early 1200s, and one family was apparently settled near Wakefield from c1330. The expansion into Bradford may have taken place via Ovenden.

1332 Thomas de Kent (Thorne) WCR
1402 John de Kent (Halifax) Clay
1483 William Kent (Ovenden) YD
1524 John Kent (Bradford) SR

Kitchen, Kitchin, Kitching

Although it has more than one family origin the surname is often distinctive in its own locality. It was clearly occupational in origin but may have denoted a man responsible for a kitchen rather than just one who worked there. Often, of course, the kitchen was a building situated away from the dwelling house at the time the surname became hereditary. Much of the expansion in Bradford and Leeds came from a family established in Eccleshill, but other Kitchens lived in and around Skipton.

1355 Thomas de Kechin (Eccleshill) YD
1467 John Kychyn (Eccleshill) YD
1545 Richard Kechyn (Eccleshill) SR
1773 John Kitchen otherwise Kitching QS

Knowles

There are numerous minor place-names derived from Old English 'cnoll' (i.e. a rounded hillock) and the surname appears to have had several origins. It is recorded in 1343 in Bradford, and expanded there in the 1600s, but there is no obvious local origin. The Knowleses recorded in the area from c1500 may therefore have been branches of a family prominent in parts of Staincliffe Wapentake to the north from the 13th century, particularly in Ribblesdale, Malham and Littondale. The identification of the place-name responsible for this surname is difficult but it is significant that a document of 1305 links Rayner de Knol with Hellifield, Arncliffe and 'the manor of Knol', possibly a reference to part of Newton in Bowland.

c1250 Richard de Cnol (Sawley) YAS 87
1473 Thomas Knoll (Long Preston) YAS 132
1519 James Knols (Halifax) Clay
1558 William Knowles (Long Preston) WYR
1641 Roger Knolls (Bradford) Prot R

Lancaster

From the county town of Lancaster. The surname is recorded from the 14th century in York and Wakefield but probably arrived in Bradford from Bowland where it was established c1500. There may have been some confusion with Longster.

1522 James Lancastre (Paythorne) LB
1539 Richard Lancaster (Bradford) MR
1641 John Lancaster (Bradford) Prot R

Laycock

A prolific Bradford name. The place-name Laycock (i.e. small stream) is in the Domesday Book and refers to the small settlement at Oakworth near Keighley. Earlier, however, it must have been the name of the beck nearby. The family's earliest generations are not well documented, but by c1500 the surname was well established in Airedale and from there found its way into Bradford.

1379 John de Laccokk (Keighley) PTY
1510 Thomas Lakok (Keighley) MR
1539 Christopher Lacok (Manningham) MR

Leach, Leech

The origin here is in doubt. It could have referred to a 'leech' or physician, but several early references show that a place-name source cannot be ruled out. In this case the meaning would be 'marshy area'. Although it is prolific now in Bradford its ramification there was late and a move from Halifax seems likely.

1297 John the Leche (Wakefield) WCR
1333 Adam de Leche (Holme) WCR
1379 John Leche (Cleckheaton) PTY
1437 John Leche (Shelf) WCR
1545 Robert Lech (Sowerby) SR
1571 Robert Leche (Bradford) CR

Ledgard, Ledger, Lidgard

This surname has a history in Bradford of at least 650 years and it is still well established there. It probably derives from a personal name brought here by the Normans, but originally of Germanic origin: it could be used by both men and women but had declined in popularity by the end of the 13th century. Curiously Reaney makes no mention of Ledgard, although he lists Legard and Ledger and gives them different origins. This was clearly possible but the Yorkshire evidence suggests that no clear distinction was made between them as surnames.

1342 John Leggard (Bradford) CR
1416 Robert Ligeard (Bradford) CR
1468 John Ledgerd (Bradford) YD
1545 Thomas Legiard (Idle) SR
1641 John Leadgard (Bradford) Prot R
1768 Mary Ledger otherwise Ledgard (Darton) QS

Leventhorpe

Apparently extinct now in Yorkshire but surviving occasionally elsewhere. It has two distinct place-name origins, one in Swillington and one in Bradford, both having the same meaning (i.e. Leofwine's outlying farmstead). The Leventhorpes of Thornton in Bradford were of some importance in the district until they acquired manors in the south and moved to Sawbridgeworth in the early 1400s. The Swillington surname never became common but did survive into Elizabeth's reign at least.

1240 John de Lowintorph YAS 25
1379 William de Lewenthorp, franklin (Thornton) PTY
1428 John Leventhorppe (Sawbridgeworth) YD
1509 Oswald Lewnethorp, lord of Horton WYD

Lightowler, Lightowlers

A common Bradford name although it originates in Lancashire. The hamlet of Lightollers (i.e. light-alders) is in Rochdale close to the boundary with Halifax parish and the family named Lightollers held land in that district for nearly four centuries. Occasionally during that period (1246-c1640) the surname found its way into the Calder Valley and other parts of Yorkshire, and by the 17th century was well established in both Halifax and Elland. In the early 1700s one branch of the family settled at Royds Hall and subsequently Lightowler became one of the most prominent surnames in the Low Moor/Wibsey area. Ironically it is rare now in Lancashire although a branch of the family was still living near Chorley in the 19th century.

1309 Magge de Ligholleres (Sowerby) WCR
1422 Ralph Lightollers (Rastrick) WCR
1577 William Lyghtoulers (Halifax) PR
1641 James Lightowlers (Elland) Prot R

Liley, Lilley

A complicated surname and Reaney has demonstrated that it has several possible origins. In the West Riding it appears to be from the French 'del isle' (i.e. island), a derivation which escaped both Reaney and Smith, and the Liley family was prominent in Mirfield and Kirkheaton from the 12th century. They gave their name to Liley Hall, on the boundary between the two parishes, and this was the family home into the 1490s. Even after this date the surname was found in Kirkheaton, but it seems likely that either then or earlier migration into Birstall and Bradford had taken place. There is no proof yet of such a move but certain circumstantial evidence supports the theory. c.f. Denby, Ledgard, Northrop.

1175-85 Ralph de Insula (Kirkheaton) EYCh.
1331 Juliana del Ylhe (Mirfield) YD
1415-33 William Lyle/Lylee/Lylegh (Mirfield) WB
1493 William Lyley (Liley Place) Dodsworth
1539 John Lilee (Wyke), Thomas Lille (Wilsden) MR
1586-92 Thomas Lilie/Lillie (Birstall) PR

Lister

Occupational in origin; the regional word for the man in charge of the dyehouse. It has several local origins but the earliest significant ramification was in Baildon. Other families lived in Bradford itself and Halifax.

1338 John le Litster (Bradford) CR
1379 John Lyster (Baildon), 'tinctor' PTY
1427 Richard Lytstar (Baildon) YD
1524 William Lyster (Baildon) SR

Longbottom

Very common in Bradford. It derives from Longbottom (i.e. long-valley bottom) a locality in Warley near Halifax. Part of the waste there was being taken in after 1300 and Adam of Warley, for example, gave '12d for two acres at Longbothem' in 1308. The surname is mentioned soon afterwards and it remained in the township for centuries. In the 1440s the Longbottoms were linked by marriage to the Rushworths of Coley and, possibly as a result of this, Northowram became a second point of ramification. In 1616 William Longbottom was a tenant of the Rookes family at Royds Hall.

1332 Richard del Longbothom Warley) WCR
1442 Richard Longbothom (Warley) WCR
1524 Richard Longbothome (Warley) SR
1530 Edward Longebothome (Northowram) YD

Longster

A rare name now but formerly well established in Skipton and Airedale. It derives from Langscar (i.e. long-rocky slope), a locality in Malham and may have been confused with both Lancaster and Langstroth.

1379 Thomas Langsker (Conistone) PTY
1522-34 Robert Langsker/Longskerthe (Skipton) LB; WYR
1539 John Langsker (Bradford) WYR
1595-97 Gregory Langskarre/Langster (Leeds) PR

Lumby

From Lumby (i.e. grove-farm), a locality in Huddleston. In the 14th century one branch of the family moved some 16 miles due west to Pudsey and significantly this is still the one locality where the surname is frequent.

1280 Walter de Lomby (Lumby) YF
1379 Robert de Lumby (Pudsey) PTY
1475 Simon Lumby (Pudsey) CR
1545 Robert Lomby (Pudsey) SR

Machen, Machin

In Normandy and Picardy this was the regional form of the occupational 'mason' and the two spellings seem to have been interchangeable locally in earlier centuries.

c 1270 Roger Cementarius (Clayton) KM
 1325 William le Masoun (Clayton) KM
 1356 Thomas Machon (Clayton) KM
 1459 John Machon (Bowling) Th 2
 1536 William Machon (Bradford) BAS
 1641 Samuel Machin (Bradford) Prot R

Mangham

A possible variant of Manningham. There are precedents for this type of development e.g. Hemingbrough, Hembrough. A quite different explanation was offered by Halliwell Sutcliffe in *Striding Dales*.

 1672 John Mangham (Leeds) HT
 1685 Simon Mangham (Hebden) Hoyle

Manningham See also **Mangham**

From Manningham in Bradford. The place-name is a difficult one but has been explained by Smith as 'Maegen's homestead'. Although the surname occurs often enough in early Bradford records, and survived in South Yorkshire into the late 16th century at least, most of its history since c1600 has been outside the county.

 1240 Matthew de Mainghama YAS 25
 1342 Robert Manyngham (Bradford) BAS
 1412 Thomas Manyngham (Manningham) CR
 1585 Janet Maningham (Doncaster) PR

Margereson, Margerison, Margerrison, Marjerison, Marjerrison See also **Jerrison** and **Margetson**

Margerison and its variants have a well documented history in Birstall and Tong back to the 16th century. Curiously the evidence there suggests that it might have developed as an alias of Margetson and no link with by-names of the type quoted by Reaney has been established.

 1411 John Margetson (Wyke) Bradford CR
 1545 John Margretson (Drighlington) SR
 1584 John Margetson (Drighlington) PR
 1587 William Margerison (Tong) Tempest

Margetson

The original form of Margereson. It is rare now, but was the family name of the Archbishop of Armagh whose origins were in Drighlington. His will shows that by 1678 his relatives were living as far afield as Leicestershire and Cambridgeshire.

Marshall

The Old French word for a farrier or shoeing smith. It had numerous origins. Its frequency in the town by 1641 probably owed something to migration from villages such as Bingley and Yeadon where Marshall was already well established in 1545.

 1342 John Marschall (Bradford) CR
 1421 John Marshall (Bradford) CR
 1539 Richard Marschall (Manningham) MR

Maud, Maude

A prolific West Riding name, which ramified in Halifax parish in the period 1316-1545, but was also common in parts of Lower Wharfedale and Airedale. It appears to have no connection locally with Matilda/Maude as suggested by Reaney and in its earliest history, dating from c1150, was written 'de Mohaut' or 'de Monte Alto' (i.e.

high hill). The hill in question has not been identified and may be in this country or in France, but it is worth noting that the forms of the Yorkshire surname are identical with those of the Flintshire place-name Mold.

1316 William of Monte Alto (Warley) WCR
1350 John Mahaud (Warley) WCR
1483 John Mawde (Halifax) Clay
1529 John Mawde (Manningham) YF
1545 Edward Mawde (Warley) SR
1585 Arthur Mawhaut alias Mawde (Riddlesden) YAS 135

Maufe See Muff

When the history of the Bradford store Brown, Muff and Co. was written in 1964 it was stated that members of the Muff family, 'reverted, in 1909, to an older form of their surname — Maufe'. The only obvious evidence for such a name locally is an isolated by-name of the late 13th century.

1297 John Maufe (Hipperholme) WCR

Metcalf, Metcalfe

This famous Yorkshire surname has been much discussed but its meaning is still uncertain. Sir Anthony Wagner suggested that it derived from a hill called the 'Calf', whereas Reaney judged it to be a nickname, basing his theory on a postulated term 'mete-cealf' (i.e. a calf fattened for meat). Weekley's view was that it should be interpreted almost literally as 'mead or meadow calf'. In fact only one reference to the surname before 1400 has been noted and all the theories are based on this isolated spelling. In the 15th century the Metcalfes' home was at Nappa in Wensleydale and the name's dramatic expansion there coincided with the family's increased status and prestige. They also acquired important estates in Craven from the Hartlingtons and by the early 1500s Metcalfes were settled throughout the Western Dales. It was already a common surname in Bradford by 1641 when James Metcalfe, esquire, headed the Protestation Returns.

1301 Adam Medecalf (Bainbridge) SR
1606 Christopher Metcalfe (Bradford) WYR

Midgeley, Midgley

The place-name Midgley (i.e. midge-infested clearing) occurs several times in Yorkshire but the source of this family name is almost certainly Midgley in Halifax parish. It first occurs in the Bradford area in the 14th century and by 1545 was widely distributed from Clayton to Haworth. It is now one of Bradford's most prolific surnames.

1274 John de Migeley (Halifax) WCR
1354 John de Miggelai (Oxenhope) CR
1412 Thomas Myggelay (Bradford) CR
1539 William Mygley (Allerton) MR

Milner

The north country form of miller — probably corn miller. It has many origins and there were important ramifications in Bingley and Skircoat.

1342 Richard le Milner (Bradford) CR
1379 Roger Milner (Bowling) PTY
1422 William Milner (Bradford) CR
1539 John Milner (Bradford) MR

Mitchell

From the colloquial form of Michael used in the Middle Ages. It has numerous origins but locally the most prolific family was in Heptonstall.

1348 Henry Michel (Bradford) CR
1379 William Michell (Allerton) PTY
1421 John Mitchell of Allerton (Bradford) CR
1524 John Michell (Haworth) SR

Moore

Much of the West Riding moorland has been cleared over the centuries and the wide distribution of 'moor' as a place-name element is evidence of this. The surname has several origins and one particularly prolific family was at Rothwell. In the Bradford area early surnames are recorded in both Haworth and Shipley.

1342 Agnes of the Moor (Bradford) BAS
1379 William del More (Haworth) PTY
1412 Robert de More (Haworth) CR
1545 William Moore (Haworth) SR

Mortimer

Ralph de Mortemer held lands in York-shire at the time of the Domesday survey and the surname is referred to afterwards at frequent intervals. Nevertheless it has not been possible to link this prominent Norman family with Mortimers settled in Bradford from c1300. This family's main property was at Scholemoor in Horton, a territory which curiously appears to have formed part of the Saviles' manor of Hunsworth. By 1545 there were Mortimers in Horton, Clayton and Thornton and subsequently the name has become prolific in Bradford and Cleckheaton.

1310 Thomas de Mortimer (Clayton) KM
1412 Thomas Mortimer (Horton) CR
1488 John Mortymer (Horton) YD
1545 Thomas Mortymer (Horton) SR

Muff See also Maufe

A surname now concentrated in the Bradford area and closely associated with the town for nearly 350 years. Its history before c1650 is far from clear but it is thought to derive from the Middle English 'maugh' (i.e. a relative by marriage). This word was still used in the 16th century to embrace all members of the family: 'Robert Whyttakerres, John his son and oder mo unknown' (1535). If this interpretation is correct the surname may have reached Bradford via Leeds. Certainly the pronunciations and spellings of Watmough/Watmuff lend support to this theory.

1558 Margaret Moygh (Rothwell) Th 27
1572 Edward Moughte (Leeds) PR
1648 John Muff (Bradford) PR
1672 James Maugh (Leeds) HT

If this name has the same origin as Maw (see Reaney) then its earlier history may go back to York via Harewood and Bolton Percy.

1322 William Maw (York) FY
1431 Thomas Magh (York) FY
1520 William Maw alias Robynson (Bolton Percy) WYR
1560 Humphrey Mawe alias Robynson (Harewood) WYR

Murgatroyd, Murgitroyd

Usually said to mean 'Margaret's clearing', but this interpretation is based largely on the 1379 example of the surname. Other spellings suggest that the first element may have been 'moor gate' (i.e. moor road) and there are similar minor place-names which lend credibility to such a derivation. e.g. 1331 le Moregatehirst (Smith). The locality lay in Warley and was later re-named Hollins. It was still one of the homes of the Murgatroyd family in the 17th century but by then the surname had ramified successfully and was well established in Airedale and Bradford.

1371 John de Morgaterode (Warley) HAS
1379 John Mergretrode (Warley) PTY
1430 Thomas Moregaterode (Warley) WCR
1517 William Murgatrode (Warley) Clay

1524 John Morgatrowyd (Bingley) SR
1571 Edmond Murgateroyde (Bradford) CR

Naylor

Prolific in and around Bradford (i.e. maker of iron nails). In 1274, for example, Richard le Neyler was allowed 'to dig for sea-coals for forging'. Although the surname has numerous origins over a wide area its early distribution is likely to reflect the incidence of iron working. This covers much of the West Riding and examples of Naylor occur in at least seven different villages in 1379. Locally there were families established in Birstall and Heptonstall and if the Naylors living in Bradford in the 1500s do not originate there, they are likely to have come from one or other of these neighbouring areas.

1379 Robert Nayler (Cleckheaton) PTY
1524 Thomas Nayller (Cleckheaton) SR
1539 Richard Naler (Wyke) MR

Netherwood

The surname has a very long history in the West Riding and seems certain to derive from a minor place-name (i.e. lower wood). There is no obvious Yorkshire source so it is possible that Netherwoods in Bowland (1379) took their name from a locality in Whalley parish. Much of the family's early history was in Airedale, and they were substantial landholders in Kildwick in the 1400s. By c1450, however, the surname had spread to Eccleshill and Farsley and it maintained its Bradford connections for centuries. It never became very common in the town and eventually ramified in the Fartown area of Huddersfield.

1379 Adam Nethyrwood (Carleton in Craven) PTY
1449 William Netherwood (Eccleshill) BAS
1545 George Nederwood (Idle) SR
1641 Samuel Netherwood (Bradford) Prot R

Nettleton

From Nettleton Hill (i.e. nettle-farmstead) a locality in the old township of Quarmby (now Longwood). The family held this property from c1280 to 1563, but appear to have lived in Thornhill from c1430, and Gledholt before that. It was a move which still affects the distribution of the surname and which no doubt accounted for its early ramification in Birstall and Tong. Although it has never become common in Bradford itself it was prominent in East Bierley and Wyke and still survives in that area.

1284 Thomas de Nettelton (Quarmby) WCR
1386 William de Nettylton (Quarmby) WCR
1457 John Netilton (Tong) WYR
1545 Richard Nettilton (Wyke) SR

Newall

The place-name New Hall is common and the surname could have several origins. The Bradford family took its name from Newhall in Bowling, but the evidence is incomplete and there may have been confusion with Newell.

1357 Robert de Newall (North Bierley) YD
1441 John Newall (Heaton) Th 6
1620 John Newall (Horton) WYR

Newby

Well established in Bradford and Leeds. It derives from one or more of the eight Yorkshire places named Newby (i.e. new-village). The Bradford family is first referred to in the early 16th century but where they came from is uncertain. There were Newbys in Leeds in the 1400s and others at Church Fenton.

1426 Thomas Newby (Church Fenton) WYR
1445 Thomas Nuby (Leeds) Th
1524-37 Thomas Nubie/Newb(y) (Bradford) SR; WYR
1641 William Newby (Bradford) Prot R

Newell

Probably for Neville, an important Birstall family which derived its name from a place in France.

1274 Geoffrey de Neville WCR
1379 John Neuyll (Liversedge) PTY
1488 John Neville/Newell (Liversedge) SS 57
1559-60 John Newell/Nevell (Birstall) PR
1596 Thomas Newell (Bradford) PR

Nichol(s), Nicholl(s)

From Nichol, the colloquial form of Nicholas. It has numerous origins including one in Elland.

1379 John Nichol (Elland) PTY
1498 Richard Nicholl (Southowram) YD
1545 William Nycols (Southowram) SR
1612 John Nicholls (Horton) WYD

Northend, Northen, Northin, Northing

The surname had its origin in Northowram and was relatively common there in the 16th and 17th centuries. In the writings of the Coley minister, Oliver Heywood, the spelling by c1700 was often 'Northen'. It cannot be traced to a particular place-name but almost certainly referred to a settlement at the north end of the ridge which gave Northowram its name. Northend is now rare in the West Riding and Northin is almost exclusively a Bradford name.

1307 Thomas del Northend (Northowram) WCR

1456 John Northend (Southowram) TN
1524 John Northend (Northowram) SR
1545 John Northend (Manningham) SR
1611 Martin Northen (Clayton) WYR

Northrop

There is a Northorpe in the East Riding but the local name derives from Northorpe (i.e. north-secondary settlement), a locality in Mirfield. It is principally a Bradford surname now as the result of an early move from Mirfield to Manningham by one branch of the family, c.f. Ledgard, Denby etc. The surname is also well established now in Cambridgeshire, c.f. Leventhorpe.

1297 Thomas del Norththorpe WCR
1342 Thomas Northorp (Manningham) BAS
1422 William Norththorp (Bradford) CR
1545 John Northrope (Manningham) SR

Norton

Norton (i.e. north-farmstead) is a common English place-name and occurs in all three Yorkshire Ridings. However it occurs only once in the West Riding, as the name of a township ten miles east of Wakefield, and a surname derived from it is recorded in the 12th century. Subsequently the surname flourished in the Leeds/Wakefield area, although it cannot be assumed that all these families shared a common origin, and by the 1500s it was established in Cleckheaton. This is, therefore, one possible source of the Nortons who became numerically important in Bradford in the 17th century.

1296 Agnes de Norton (Sandal) WCR
1524 Simon Norton (Sandal) SR
1559 Robert Norton (Birstall) PR
1641 Robert Norton (Bradford) Prot R

Nunwick, Nunweek, Numweek

From Nunwick (i.e. nun-dairy-farm) near Ripon. The surname is recorded from the 13th century but has never been common. It may have arrived in Bradford from Bowland for in the early 1500s the Nunwicks were tenants of Sir Richard Tempest at Bracewell.

   1379 Robert de Nunwik (Nunwick) PTY
   1524 William Nunweyke (Bracewell) SR
   1641 Richard Nunwicke (Bradford) Prot R

Nussey

From a locality in Appletreewick in Burnsall parish. The family remained in the parish for centuries and when William Nussie died in Bradford in 1521 he left 3s. 4d towards the upkeep of Burnsall church. A rare name now.

   1379 John de Nussay (Appletreewick) PTY
   1473 Thomas Nussay (Appletreewick) YAS 132
   1545 John Nussey (Horton) SR
   1641 William Nussey (Bradford) Prot R

Oates

A prolific West Riding surname derived from the personal name 'Otes'. This was brought to England by the Normans, remained popular in Calderdale in the 14th century, and was even in occasional use in the 1600s. Locally the surname ramified in Southowram and in its early history alternated with 'Oateson'.

   1355 Otes de Haldeworth (Ovenden) WCR
   1379 Robert Otesson/John Hotes (Southowram) PTY
   1439 Robert Otes alias Oteson (Halifax) HAS
   1491 Gilbert Otes (Southowram) YD
   1545 Brian Ottes (Northowram) SR
   1598 Walter Otes (Ogden) WYR

Obank, O'Bank, Woabank

These uncommon names are variants of Ewbank, which seems likely to derive from Yewbank in Cumberland, or possibly Ewbank in Westmorland. The surname may have reached Bradford indirectly for it was well-known in York in the 15th and 16th centuries.

   1464 William Hughbank (York) FY
   1522-24 William Hewbank/Howbanke (York) SS; SR
   1647 Henry Obanke (Barkisland) PR
   1679 Alice Owbanke/Obancke/Wobancke (Selby) SS

Oddy, Hoddy

From the Scandinavian personal name 'Oddi', which was still occasionally used in Yorkshire in the 13th century. In this case the progenitor can be identified as a man holding land in Rimington in Bowland and this village continued as the family's main home for several centuries. In the 16th century the name spread to Airedale and by 1600 it was well established in a number of places close to Bradford.

   1280-90 Hoddi of Gasegill (Rimington) YAS 56
   1311 Roger Oddy (Rimington) YAS 56
   1379 John Odde (Rimington) PTY
   1510 James Oddy (Rimington) MR
   1545-62 Richard Odde/Hoddye (Guiseley) SR; WYR

Ogden

A prolific Bradford name. In this case, as in several others, the place-name is found both in Yorkshire and in Lancashire and it is uncertain how many origins the surname has. The Bradford surname is well documented from the late 1400s and may derive from Ogden (i.e. oak tree-valley), a locality in Ovenden. However the evidence before that is still unsatisfactory and the isolated reference of 1309, used by Smith as evidence of the place-name, almost certainly refers to a trespasser from Rochdale.

1309 Hancock de Okedene (Sowerby) WCR
1472 John Okeden (Bradford) YD
1545 Richard Ogden (Bowling) SR

Ormondroyd, Ormonroyd, Ormandroyd, Ormanroyd See also Halmonroyd

In the past surname aliases were much more common than has generally been recognised. They took different forms, but one common type developed when the surname lost a syllable, in much the same way that 'bus' and 'telly' have replaced omnibus and television in colloquial speech. Such abbreviated forms are usually seen as variants of the surname, but in the case of Ormondroyd the abbreviation was in general use over a period of nearly 500 years and the full surname was rarely employed. Ormondroyd derives from a minor locality meaning 'Hamond's royd or clearing' (possibly 'Hamondesrode' in Wibsey [1307], incorrectly recorded by Smith) and the family lived in Horton in the 14th century. After that, however, it seems to have survived as 'Hawmond' until comparatively recent times, finally reverting to the full form in the 19th century in at least one branch of the family. The modern conventional spelling may have been influenced by the Lancashire surname Ormerod, or even by the ducal title Ormonde. As Hammond is also prolific in Bradford it is likely that this sometimes shares the same origin.

1350 William de Hamundrode (Bradford) CR
1379 William Hawmunrode (Horton) PTY
1509 Gilbert Hawmound (Horton) Misc. MSS. B/54
1545 Miles Hawmond (Horton) SR
1571 William Awmonde (Bradford) CR

Padgett, Patchett

These surnames are both prolific now in Bradford. It is usual to treat them separately, with Padgett explained as a diminutive of Page and Patchett as a diminutive of Patch (See Reaney). Locally, however, it is not possible to separate them, although the early manorial evidence favours a derivation from one of the Middle English meanings of 'patch'. For example in the court rolls for Sowerbyshire there is reference to John Pachet (1352) and Richard Pachet (1374): in the Poll Tax these men, or their descendants, were entered as John and Richard Paget, possibly by a clerk who was not a local man. It was nevertheless a spelling which would occur more frequently as time passed. The major expansion of the surname was in the neighbouring villages of Warley and Midgley and, despite occasional references to it in Bradford from the early 1400s, the first clear evidence of a family resident there occurs in the 1641 returns for Haworth.

1403 Richard Pachet (Sowerbyshire) WCR
1472 Richard Pagett (Sowerbyshire) WCR
1563 Richard Paget/Pacchett (Warley) PR
1572-73 Richard Patchett/Pagett (Bradford) CR

Parkinson

'Son of Parkin or Perkin', a diminutive of Per (see Pearson). The surname has several origins but it was particularly common in Airedale and reached Bradford in the 16th century.

1379 Robert Perkynson (Marton) PTY
1410 Laurence Perkynson (Bingley) YD
1522 John Parkynson (Steeton) LB
1543 Robert Parkinson (Steeton) SR
1588 Richard Parkinson (Shipley) WYR

Patchett See **Padgett**

Pearson

'Son of Per(s)', the French form of Peter, which persisted into the 17th century at least, e.g. 1554 Pers, son of Gilbert Hilele of Halifax (PR). The surname is extremely prolific locally and no doubt has many origins. It was already well established in Birstall and Bradford by c1540.

1342 Thomas Pierson (Bradford) CR
1415 Lawrence Peresson (Bradford) CR
1485 William Pierson (Brighouse) CR
1545 James Person (Bradford/ Cleckheaton) SR

Phillips

From Philip, a common personal name in the Middle Ages, and the surname must have had numerous origins. Nevertheless it was not common in the West Riding and the small number taxed in Bradford and Sowerbyshire in 1545 may have shared a common origin.

1342 Henry Philipp (Bradford) CR
1402 Henry Philippe (Horton) YD
1539 Thomas Phillip (Thornton) MR
1641 Robert Phillip (Clayton) Prot R

Pickard

Probably for a man from Picardy, although Reaney has examples of it as a personal name in the 13th century. It has numerous origins but is particularly common in and around Bradford. There were families with this name in the 14th century both in Lower Wharfedale and the Tong/Calverley area.

1343 Hugh Pikard (Tong) YD
1435 Hugh Pickard (Baildon) WYD
1539 Richard Pykhard (Bradford) MR

Pickles See also **Pighills**

There are several hundred families with this surname in and around Bradford and the ramification can be traced to Haworth, where the surname was already numerous by 1545. Although its history in that part of Bradford goes back to the 13th century there is still no categoric proof of its origin and meaning. In fact the evidence is conflicting: on the one hand it points to a surname derived from a locality 'piked ley' (i.e. clearing with corners, or pointed clearing); on the other hand it suggests a connection with the common Middle English word 'pightel', meaning a small enclosure. It could be that two quite distinct names, occurring in the same area, were confused at a very early date, or more probably that the surname originated in the minor place-name and was repeatedly confused with 'pightel'. If this supposition is correct it is ironic that all connection with the place-name was lost by c1600.

1252 Alexander of Pikedel' (Wilsden) BAS
1346 William del Piktelegh (Bradford) CR
1379 Richard de Pighkeleys (Haworth) PTY
1379 Stephen de Pykedleghes (Haworth) PTY
1545 Laurence Bightley (sic) (Haworth) SR
1588 Henry Pighley (Haworth) SR
1354 Elias de Pighels (Bradford) CR
1414 John Pighyls (Haworth) CR
1478 John Pyghyls (Haworth) TN
1539 Laurence Pyghills (Haworth) MR
1641 Edward Pickles (Haworth) Prot R

Pighills See **Pickles**

This relatively uncommon name preserves the form of Pickles which was usual in the period 1400-1600.

1755 Richard Pickles otherwise Pighells (Wakefield) QS

Pollard

Pollard was first recorded in Bradford in the 1400s and is now prolific there. Its precise origins and meaning are far from clear for the surname was already frequent and widely distributed in Yorkshire in the 12th and 13th centuries. Such families seem unlikely to share a common ancestry, but the Bradford Pollards may have had close connections with a family which ramified in the Birstall area.

1416 William Pollerd (Brighouse) CR
1437 William Pollard (Tong) YD
1459 John Pollerd (Newhall) Th 2
1539 Nicholas Pollerd (Wyke) MR

Priestley

From Priestley (i.e. priest-clearing), a locality in Hipperholme which continued to be the family's main home for well over a century. However, very early in the 1400s, they appear to have moved into the Elland area and by 1545 the surname was established in Stainland, Sowerby and Halifax. It eventually became prolific in Bradford and probably arrived there c1600.

13thc. Robert de Prestel' (Hipperholme) WCR
1379 John de Presteley (Hipperholme) PTY
1419 Robert de Preesteleye (Barkisland) YD
1545 Henry Prestley (Sowerby) SR
1627 Margaret Preistley (Bradford) WYR

Pyrah

The first references to Pyrah occur in the 18th century in Bradford and neighbouring parishes to the south and this is still the one area in which the surname is at all common. There is no clear evidence linking it with any other part of England, or with a better known name in Yorkshire and its origin and meaning remain a mystery.

1703 Joshua Pyrah (Bradford) PR

1736 Abraham Pyerah (Northowram) NC
1784 Benjamin Pyrah (Birstall) PR

Raistrick, Rastrick, Restrick(?)

From Rastrick (i.e. resting-place-track), a township in Elland chapelry, and the home of the family for over one hundred years. They then moved further to the North and there are early references to the name in Northowram and Eccleshill. It remained uncommon until relatively late but when it ramified the expansion was in Airedale, from Calverley to Rawdon, and the surname is now almost exclusively associated with that area and Bradford. The conventional spelling (i.e. Raistrick), reflects the colloquial pronunciation and emphasises the break with the place-name.

1272 John de Rastrick (Rastrick) WCR
1379 Roger de Rastrig (Northowram) PTY
1433 Henry de Rastryk (Eccleshill) WYD
1475 John Rastryk (Pudsey) CR
1563 Thomas Raystrick (Guiseley) WYR
1641 Anthony Restrike (Calverley) Prot R

Ramsden

Probably from Ramsden near Holmfirth. The meaning could be either 'ram-valley' or 'wild garlic-valley'. The Ramsdens were tenants of Wakefield manor and lived in or near Holmfirth in the 14th century. They appear to have moved to Barkisland in the same manor before c1400 and the surname then ramified in Elland. It is recorded in the Bradford area in the early 1500s.

1539 Gilbert Ramysden (Bradford) MR
1641 William Ramsden (Bradford) Prot R

Rastrick See Raistrick

Rawson

'Son of Raw', probably a form of Ralph. It could have several origins but one well documented family has a long history in Bradford itself and played a prominent role in the town's development. There were also Rawsons in Bingley and Keighley in the early 1500s who may not share the same family origin.

1357 John son of Ralph (Bradford) CR
1359 John Rawson (Bradford) CR
1426 Thomas Rawson (Bradford) Th 6
1488 William Rauson (Bradford) YD
1545 John Rawson (Bradford) SR

Rayner, Raynor

From Rainer or Reiner, a personal name brought to England by the Normans and popular in the West Riding in the Middle Ages. One prominent bearer of the name was Reiner le Fleming, whose family held the manor of Clifton, and who c1180 confirmed the grant of Kirklees to the nuns there. Other members of the Fleming family were also called Reiner and it is tempting to see a link between them and the Rayners who were eventually so numerous in places adjoining Clifton, such as Rastrick, Hartshead and Liversedge. The surname occurred twenty-four times in the local subsidy roll of 1545, most of them in that precise area. Lionel Rayner who later lived in Eccleshill seems certain to share the same family origins.

1274 John, son of Reyner (Rastrick) WCR
1314 Thomas, son of John Reiner (Rastrick) WCR
1350 John, son of Thomas Rayner (Rastrick) WCR
1446 William Rayner (Liversedge) YD
1545 Lionel Rayner (Liversedge) SR
1592 Lionel Rayner (Eccleshill) WCR

Rhodes, Royds

Prolific and widely distributed in the West Riding. It derives from a Middle English word meaning a clearing, which gave rise to numerous minor place-names in the period 1150-1350. The early spelling 'Rodes' was diphthongised in West Riding dialect and gave way to 'Roides', or 'Roydes' in the 1500s. Curiously, however, the conventional spelling of the surname later became Rhodes, perhaps influenced by clergymen who knew of the island of that name. It is a surname with several quite independent origins but an important local source was a territory in North Bierley, marked now by Royds Hall.

1340 Thomas de Rodes (Bradford) CR
1435 William Rodes (Bradford) WYR
1527 William Roydes (Tong) Tempest
1561 Richard Rodes (North Bierley) YD
1637 William Rhodes/Roydes (Birstall) PR

Riddlesden, Riddlesdin, Ruddlesden, Ruddleston

A family called Riddlesden was recorded in Birstall parish from c1500, but its earlier history is very obscure. The surname no doubt derives from Riddlesden (i.e. Rethel's valley) near Keighley and it occurred there as early as c1200. Between those two dates, however, the surname is seldom encountered, except in the 1370s with references to it at Yeadon, Mirfield and Methley. After c1540 the history of the family in Wyke and North Bierley is much better documented, particularly at High Fearnley, and during the 17th century they were accorded the status of gentry. It was eventually in the Dewsbury/Wakefield area that the surname became relatively common, and there too that Ruddlesden became accepted as the more usual spelling.

1379 Thomas Ridilsden (Mirfield)
PTY
1516 William Rylsdon (sic)
(Birstall) Th
1571 John Rydilsden (Bradford) CR
1606 John Riddlesden (Wyke) WYD
1665-66 John Riddlesden/Ruddles-
den (Wyke) PR

Rishworth, Rishforth See Rushworth

From Rishworth near Elland. The more
usual spelling of the surname now is
Rushworth. The fact that this spelling
is found in Airedale and Wharfedale
suggests that it has been influenced by
the place-name Ryshworth, which was
originally 'Rishford'.

1612 William Rishforth (Leeds) Th

Robertshaw, Robinshaw, Robshaw

From Robertshaw (i.e. Robert's-copse),
a locality near Heptonstall. One branch
of the family moved over the ridge
into the Thornton area of Bradford,
probably before 1500, and the surname
soon became numerous there. Because
the personal name Robert was colloquially 'Rob' or 'Robin' the surname
also developed the variants Robshaw
and Robinshaw and this latter form
could even be confused with Robinson.

1422 Richard Robertschawe
(Sowerbyshire) WCR
1502 Edward Robertschaw (Bradford) SS
1585 Edward Robertshay (Thornton)
WYD
1669 Henry Robinshaw/Robinson
(Oakenshaw) PR
1732 Henry Robshaw alias Robertshaw (Soothill) QS

Robinson

'Son of Robin', a diminutive of
Robert based on the pet form Rob. In
1545 there were Robinsons in at least
five local townships, possibly all
branches of a family living in Thornton
in the early 1400s.

1421 John Robynson (Thornton) YD
1545 John Robynson (Thornton) SR
1641 John Robinson (Thornton)
Prot R

Robshaw See Robertshaw

Rodley

From Rodley (i.e. Rotholf's clearing),
a locality near Leeds. There are occasional references to the Rodleys of
Rodley into the 1400s, but it is clear
that the family had other significant
holdings in the same area, notably in
Pudsey and Calverley. From c1250
to c1460 they seem not to have moved
far beyond these villages but in the
next eighty or so years, possibly
through their role as free tenants of
Kirkstall Abbey, they expanded considerably, becoming involved in com-
merce in Pontefract and Wakefield and
entering the merchant class in Bradford. John Rodley acquired the abbey
property at Low Moor known as Park
House and soon merited the title
'gentleman'. However, he moved c1570
to Lofthouse Hall, another of his
important properties, and the surname
became much less prominent in the
town.

c1250 Walter de Rothele (Calverley?)
Th 6
1379 Robert de Rothelay (Pudsey)
PTY
1459 Edward Rothelay (Calverley)
Th 2
1545 John Rodley (North Bierley)
SR
1641 Tempest Rodley (Bradford)
Prot R

Rookes, Rooks

These surnames are relatively common
in other parts of England and have
been discussed at length by Reaney.
One origin not mentioned in that
account is the locality Rookes near
Norwood Green, thought by Smith to

mean a 'rick' or heap of fuel or grain. The surname is recorded as early as 1187 and the family remained at Rookes at least until c1500. However, Richard Rokes settled at Royds Hall c1450 and his descendants were prominent members of the local gentry well into the 18th century. There were other branches of the family in Idle and Bradford but it is not certain if their descendants are among those who now bear the name locally.

1275 Jordan del Rokes (Hipperholme) WCR
1397 John Rokes (Hipperholme) YD
1458 Richard Rokes (Royds Hall) WCR
1545 Edward Rookes (Idle) SR
1641 Jeremie Rookes (Bradford) Prot R

Royds See **Rhodes**

Ruddlesden, Ruddleston
See **Riddlesden**

Rushworth, Rushforth, Rushfirth
See also **Rishworth**

A prolific but complicated surname. It derives from Rishworth (i.e. rush-enclosure), a territory in Elland chapelry. There is, however, a second place-name, Ryshworth, in Airedale which originally had the suffix 'ford' (e.g. Ryshforth 1323) and gave rise to a by-name. Its present spelling is almost certainly the result of confusion with the Elland locality or the surname derived from it, but it may in turn have helped the development of those variants with the suffix 'forth'. The surname Rushworth was originally a dialect variant but it is now the conventional spelling locally. The Rushworth family moved to Coley (Hipperholme) in the 1300s and lived at Coley Hall for over 200 years. They acquired land in many parts of Yorkshire and also in Colne in Lancashire

and the surname was soon widely distributed. Even so Bradford was at the heart of this ramification and one branch in Haworth was particularly numerous.

c1200 Elias de Rissewurdhe (Rishworth) FA
1286 Henry de Rissewrth (Rishworth) WCR
1379 Henry de Rysseworth (Hipperholme) PTY
1453 Henry Rysheworth (Hipperholme) WCR
1494 John Rissewrth (Haworth) YD
1570-73 Henry Rushworth/Ryshworthe (Halifax) PR
1768 Abraham Rusworth otherwise Rusher (Haworth) QS

Rycroft, Ryecroft
The earliest Yorkshire reference to this surname is in North Bierley and this points to a derivation from Ryecroft (i.e. rye-enclosure) in Tong. A connection between the family and the Tong area is evident as late as the 17th century, although it is far from clear whether the Rycrofts were resident there for the whole of the period. In fact the major concentration of the surname in the early 1500s was in the Kildwick and Skipton areas, some 18 miles from Tong. If these Airedale families share the same family origin, the explanation may lie in the tenurial history of the two places for parts of Kildwick were held by the Tong family of Tong in the early 1400s.

1379 Richard Rycroft (North Bierley) PTY
c1476 William Rycroft (Idle) PC
1562 Robert Rycroft (Tong) MSS 3/40

Sagar
Although occasional examples of this common Bradford surname occur in early Yorkshire records, e.g. Doncaster (1476) and Wakefield (1545), there is

no clear evidence of a local origin. McKinley described it as being well established in the 16th century 'around Whalley, Burnley and Colne' so the probability is that it reached Bradford via Bowland.

1600 James Sagar (Rimington) WYR
1614 John Sagar (Rimington) WYR
1620 Thomas Sager (Bradford) WYR
1641 James Sagar (Bradford) Prot R

Scholes

The place-name means 'shielings or sheds' and is relatively common in the West Riding, as at Scholes (Cleckheaton). The source of the Bradford surname is not certain.

1338 Thomas de Scoles (Bradford) CR
1379 Robert de Scoles (Heaton) PTY
1422 William Scoles (Heaton) CR
1545 John Scoles (Bradford) SR

Scott

A prolific name with multiple origins and meaning simply 'the Scot'. It seems to have had local origins in Haworth and Birstall, but it was also used as an alias by the Calverleys of Calverley.

1345 Nicholas Scot (Keighley), Bradford CR
1379 Adam Scotte (Haworth) PTY
1545 Robert Scott (Haworth) SR
1641 John Scot (Haworth) Prot R

Shackleton

A prolific Bradford surname. It derives from a locality in Wadsworth, originally 'Shackletonstall'. the 'tonstall' element (i.e. farmstead) is found in several neighbouring place-names e.g. Heptonstall, but it is far from clear what the prefix means. The surname expanded in Wadsworth and soon spread to Haworth where it ramified before 1545. Reaney suggested that it derived from a North Yorkshire place-name

Scackleton, but there is no evidence of a hereditary family name there.

1274 Jordan de Schakeltonstal WCR
1422 John Shakylton (Bradford) CR
1524 Richard Schakkylton (Haworth) SR
1641 Richard Schackleton (Haworth) Prot R

Sharp, Sharpe

Probably a nickname. In York, for example, William Cooper's son, who was a sawyer by occupation, took the surname Sharpe in 1440. The surname is prolific in Bradford, first occurring there in the 14th century, and ramifying in Horton. Several members of this family were prominent locally and Abraham Sharpe was a famous astronomer and mathematician in his day. There were other families with the same surname in the West Riding, notably at Rothwell, but there is no clear evidence of any connection.

1342 John Scharp (Bradford) BAS
1410 Thomas Scharp (Horton) CR
1488 Christopher Sharp (Horton) YD
1545 James Sharpe (Horton) SR

Shoesmith, Shucksmith, Sucksmith

Shoesmith probably originated in South Lancashire where it has been noted in the 15th and 16th centuries, but the variant forms do not always support the view that it should be interpreted literally as a maker of horse shoes. The first Yorkshire references are in the Dales e.g. Hampsthwaite (1604), but it was in the parishes to the south-west of Bradford that it eventually ramified.

1657 William Shooesmith (Hartshead) PR
1675 James Sucksmith alias Shosmith (Shelf) QS
1681-83 Thomas Showsmith/Shoosmith (Wyke) PR
1705 Joseph Sucksmith/Shucksmith (Clayton) QS

Siddall, Siddle

The surname became established in Bradford in the 17th century and could have arrived there from a number of places. For example, in the period 1540-1620, there were Siddalls who were clothiers in Wakefield and in Holbeck (Leeds). On the face of it the name should derive from Siddal (i.e. large-nook of land) in Halifax, but there is no evidence yet to confirm this and there may be a connection with the Lancashire surname Siddall, said by McKinley to be fairly common in the south of the county during the 16th and 17th centuries.

1374 Thomas de Sidale (Sowerby) WCR
1545 George Siddall (Hunslet) SR
1622 John Siddall (Holbeck) WYR

1438 Thomas Sedolles (Waddington) YD
1543 Thomas Sedayle (Waddington) SR
1545-56 John Sedall/Siddall (Wakefield) SR
1561 James Sedell (Halifax) PR

Silson

'Son of Cyll', a pet form of Cecilia. It appears to have a single origin in Littondale, and was prominent there for centuries. An early move took the surname to Gargrave (1522) and by the end of the 17th century there were Silsons in Otley, Calverley and Leeds. Later it became confused there with two other Yorkshire surnames, Silkstone and Sigston. Finally, c1700, it arrived in Bradford, which became its main home and it is now well represented in Allerton and Clayton.

1379 John Cyllson (Arncliffe) PTY
1456 Henry Sylson (Littondale) SS 130
1560 Alice Sylson (Arncliffe) WYR
1680 William Silson (Calverley) PR
1701 William Silson (Bradford) PR

Slater

There is evidence to show that stone slates were used as a roofing material locally in the Middle Ages and Slater was a common surname. Significantly there were families at Northowram and Thornton, both quarrying areas.

1379 Thomas Sclater (Thornton) PTY
1415 Geoffrey Sclater (Bradford) CR
1545 Elizabeth Slaiter (Allerton) SR

Smith

It has multiple origins including one in Bradford. In fact the first reference to the surname was to the tenant of the forge.

1342 Richard the Smyth (Bradford) BAS
1379 Thomas Smyth (Bradford) PTY
1415 John Smyth (Bradford) CR
1488 William Smyth (Manningham) YD
1537 William Smyth (Manningham) YD

Smithies

In sharp contrast to Smith this surname appears to have a limited number of origins. Although it is far from common generally it has ramified in Bradford in the last 500 years and may have arrived there from Bowland.

1379 Robert del Smethy (Rimington) PTY
1488 Thomas Smythis (Horton) YD
1522-25 Christopher Smythes/ Smedyes (Gisburn) LB; SR
1539 Christopher Smythis (Bradford) MR

Snowden, Snowdon

It has several origins but locally derives from Snowden (i.e. snow-hill) a locality in Askwith. The early expansion was in Lower Wharfedale and by c1540 there were Snowdens in Harewood, Collingham and Yeadon. It became

a common name in Bradford in the
17th century.

1260 John de Snauden (Askwith)
     Weston
1379 William Snawdon (Yeadon)
     PTY
1545 William Snawdon (Yeadon) SR
1597 Peter Snowden (Bradford) PR

Southard, Southart, Southward, Southwart See Suddards

Sowden

Although it is common in Bradford
Sowden occurs in significant numbers
in one or two other areas and the
origins and meanings are likely to be
quite distinct. Cottle derives Sowden
in Devon from a place-name meaning
'south-hill' and Reaney suggests a link
with 'soudan', the Old French word
for sultan. In the Bradford area, however, where the evidence is far from
clear cut, Sowden seems to have its
origin in a place-name meaning 'south-
valley'. The will of Robert Bolling,
proved in 1487, records a gift of lands
in 'Thornton, Headley and Sowden',
which is at the heart of the surname's
distribution in the 16th century. In
1545, for example, there was a concentration of families in Allerton,
Haworth and Keighley, with half a
dozen others in various parts of Bradford and Airedale.

1323 Robert del Southdene
     (Brighouse) WCR
1379 William de Thoweden?
     (Thornton) PTY
1510 Thomas Sowden (Keighley)
     MR
1539 John Sowden (Wilsden) MR

Speight

A very common name in Bradford and
first recorded there in the 1590s.
There were two families in the neighbourhood, one in Birstall parish and
one in Kildwick: they may have been
related at a very early date but are
quite distinct from the 14th century.
In Middle English a 'speight' was what
we now call a green woodpecker, so
the surname was almost certainly a
nickname to begin with. It is interesting to note that Speight was at times
confused with Speck for this name
also meant woodpecker and is first
recorded in Yorkshire in the early
12th century.

1297 John Specth, WCR
1379 William Speght (Gomersal)
     PTY
1545 James Speight (Gomersal) SR
1573 Humphrey Speighte (Bradford)
     CR
1641 James Speight (Bradford) Prot R
1764 Elizabeth Speight otherwise
     Speak (Long Preston) QS

Staincliffe, Stancliffe

Probably from a locality in Northowram (i.e. stone-cliff), although the
place-name occurs several times in the
West Riding. The family ramified in
Northowram and Ovenden and reached
Bradford at an early date. Now, however, the main concentrations of the
surname are in Huddersfield and
Halifax.

1274 Hugh de Stanclif (Northowram)
     WCR
1379 John de Stayneclif (North-
     owram) PTY
1530 Richard Stanclyff (Northow-
     ram) YD
1539 John Stancliffe (Clayton) MR
1641 Richard Stankliffe (Bradford)
     Prot R

Stead

From the locality Stead in Burley in
Wharfedale, rather than from Stead
in Hazlewood. The place-name probably meant 'estate' or 'farm' and it
gave rise to a surname, well-documented from the mid 13th century.
The evidence points to a single origin
locally, but there was a remarkable

early ramification and although much of it was in the Burley area, the surname soon spread to other parts of the West Riding. There were Steads in Bradford in the 1300s, but other families may have arrived there much later via Baildon and Calverley. By 1540 there were important families in both Tong and North Bierley.

1258 Isaac de la Stede (Burley) Weston
1296 William del Stede (Burley) YI
1379 Peter del Stede (Burley) PTY
1479 Robert Steed (Baildon) WYD
1537 Thomas Stede (North Bierley) WYD

Sucksmith See Shoesmith

Suddards, Suthers, Southwart, Southart, Southward, Southard(s)

The Lancashire surname Southworth (i.e. south-enclosure) is recorded in Bowland in the 14th century and other isolated examples occur in the 1400s in the urban centres of Yorkshire, e.g. York (1447), Wakefield (1460) and Ripon (1484). In the 17th century, probably as the result of a more recent and direct migration from Lancashire, Southworth occurred in several West Riding parishes and developed a fascinating range of variants, one or two of which suggest a confusion with 'south-hurst'. Few of these are common except Suddards which is now almost exclusively a Bradford name.

1641 James Southward (Erringden) Prot R
1667-69 John Sudderd/Suthers (Huddersfield) PR
1673 Jane Southerd (Sawley) Gisburn PR
1675 John Suthworth/Suthurst (Sawley) QS
1775 John Southwart (Hartshead) PR

Sugden

Probably from a locality in Haworth, although the place-name also occurs in Bingley, and there were Sugden families in both places in the 14th century. The meaning (i.e. swamp valley) is the same in either case. The surname ramified in both Bradford and Keighley in the 16th century and is now prolific.

1354 Hugh de Sugden (Haworth) CR
1379 Robert de Sugden (Haworth) PTY
1510 John Sugden (Keighley) MR
1539 Blase Sugden (Bradford) MR

Sunderland

Sunderland occurs several times as a place-name in the North of England and is thought to denote a piece of land 'sundered' from an estate or set apart from it in some particular way. The prolific local surname derives from High Sunderland in Northowram.

1274 Alcok de Sondreland (Sowerbyshire) WCR
1379 Richard de Sundirland (Northowram) PTY
1545 Richard Sonnderland (Northowram) SR
1641 Richard Sunderland (Bradford) Prot R

Sutcliffe, Sutliffe, Sutleff, Sutlieff

From Sutcliff (i.e. south-cliff/slope), a locality near Brighouse. The family had close connections with Hipperholme in the late 13th century but soon after that one branch moved to Wadsworth and ramified there. The migration into Bradford was almost certainly via Haworth: in the subsidy roll of 1545 the twenty-three Sutcliffes listed were taxed in the Heptonstall area (18) and the three Bradford townships of Haworth, Thornton and Horton.

1274 Hugh de Suthclif (Hipperholme) WCR
1379 Adam Southclif (Wadsworth) PTY
1465 Thomas Southcliff (Hepton- stall) WYR
1545 Robert Sutcliffe (Haworth) SR
1783 Jonas Sutlief (Hartshead) PR

Suthers See **Suddards**

Swaine, Swan

Reaney has shown that these names can have quite separate origins, but this need not be so locally where one family used both spellings. In their case the surname probably derives from the Scandinavian personal name Sveinn, which was popular in the West Riding in the 12th and 13th centuries, and continued to be used occasionally in the 14th. The Swaines were numerous in Horton and Idle in the 1500s and seem to have arrived in Bradford in the late 1400s. Unfortunately there is no evidence yet to say where exactly they came from, but the possibilities include places as far apart as Horbury and York.

12thc Swen de Clettona (Clayton nr Bradford) EYCh
1317 Swayn of Osset WCR
1379 John Swayn (Horbury) PTY
1487 James Swayne (Bowling) BAS
1539-45 James Swan/Swayne (Horton) MR; SR

Swift

Common and widely distributed in the West Riding. Although it has several origins much of the ramification seems to be in parts of Wakefield manor, particularly in Sowerbyshire. It was probably a nickname originally, although Reaney has shown that it could also be used as a personal name.

1307 John Swyfte (Sowerby) WCR
1379 Richard Swyft (Sowerby) PTY

1489 John Swift (Sowerby) Y Gen.
1536 Robert Swyft (Stanbury) YF
1641 Edward Swift (Bradford) Prot R

Tankard, Tancred

From a personal name brought here by the Normans. It was never very common but occurs in North Yorkshire in the 12th century. It became a surname in Boroughbridge and this appears to be the only Yorkshire origin. There is an early reference to the surname in Clayton, but the ramification was quite late. Now it is almost exclusively a Bradford area surname.

1193 Ralph filius Tankardi de Kerebi Y Pipe
1299 William Tankard (Borough- bridge) YI
1379 William Tankard (Borough- bridge) PTY
1494 William Tankerd (Borough- bridge) SS 57
1563 William Tanckurd/Tancred (Boroughbridge) YAS
1616 William Tankerd (Clayton) PR

Taylor

Only Smith is more prolific now in the West Riding and Taylor clearly has multiple origins. Despite that the evidence for a Bradford origin is unsatisfactory and the early references cannot easily be linked together. In fact, despite its frequency generally, there are notable areas where it was still uncommon in Tudor times. In 1545, for example, when the subsidy roll shows Taylor as a well established surname in Leeds, Huddersfield, Wakefield, Birstall and Otley it was rare in Bradford and absent from Halifax.

1342 Hugh Taillour (Horton) BAS
1379 John Talour (Allerton) PTY
1412 John Taillior (Manningham) CR
1463 Thomas Talyor (Bowling) WYD
1545 James Talyor (Bradford) SR

Tempest

An unusual name, probably with a single origin. It derives from the French word for a violent storm and seems likely to have been a nickname originally. However, the circumstances in which it developed are not known and there is no obvious French parallel. The family has been prominent among the Yorkshire gentry from the 12th century and by the 1300s had important estates near Skipton, notably at Bracewell and Broughton. The connection with Bradford, which was to influence the distribution of other Bowland names, began in 1497 when Richard Tempest married Rosamund Bolling and moved to Bolling Hall. The family's history there and at Tong is well documented, but other branches of the family were settled in the West Riding and the surname eventually became common in Airedale and Bradford.

1156 Roger Tempestas (Pontefract) YAS 30
1279 Roger Tempest (Hartlington) YI
1379 John Tempest (Waddington) PTY
1469 Roger Tempest (Broughton) WYR
1545 John Tempest (Bowling) SR

Terry

From a personal name discussed by Reaney. There is no evidence of a West Riding origin but c1300 there were Terrys in the North Riding and also in York where there is clear evidence of family continuity. The surname is still well known there, but in the 1500s, perhaps as a result of the city's decline, it became dispersed over a much wider area and appeared in West Riding towns such as Ripon and Doncaster. The earliest evidence in Bradford relates to a family in Bowling in the early 1600s, but their precise origin is not known.

1290 John Terry (York) YI
1390 Nicholas Terry, pewterer, (York) FY
1467 John Terry, goldsmith (York) FY
1552 Robert Tyrry, smith (York) FY
1578 William Terrie (Kirkstall) PR
1626 Marmaduke Tirrye (Bowling) WYD
1641 Edward Terry (Bradford) Prot R

Tetley, Tetlow

Some early Yorkshire surnames, e.g. 1310 John de Tetteley (Axholme), YF, are likely to derive from Tetley in Lincolnshire, but they do not seem to be linked with the surname Tetley which ramified in Birstall parish in the 16th and 17th centuries. This family name is more likely to be from Lancashire and may be connected with Tatlock. McKinley noted that it was widespread in the South of the county but could not identify the place-name source.

1343 Hugh de Tetlowe (Lancashire) Fishwick
1542-47 Seth Tetlawe/Tatlowe (Halifax) PR
1564-72 George Tetley/Tetlawe (Birstall) PR
1641 George Tetley (Birkenshaw) PR

Thomas, Thomis, Tommis

'Son of Thomas', a type of patronymic which has multiple origins but is rare in the West Riding. The surname is first recorded in Bradford in the early 1500s and probably came from Wadsworth. The variants are well established in Bradford but uncommon elsewhere.

1379 John Thomas (Wadsworth) PTY
1524 William Thomas (Wadsworth) SR
1539 Christopher Thomas (Bradford) MR
1635 Samuel Thomisse (Bradford) PR
1703 Robert Thomis/Tomis (Elland) PR

Thornton

The place-name Thornton is common in the North of England and particularly so in Yorkshire where it occurs at least sixteen times. The surname is likely, therefore, to have numerous origins and this can be inferred from its wide distribution at an early date. In Bradford, where it is exceptionally prolific, it derives from Thornton (i.e. thorn-farmstead) in Bradford-dale and is first recorded in the 12th century. By 1545 it was well distributed throughout the parish and among the commonest names there in 1641.

 1342 Roger de Thornton (Allerton) BAS
 1466 William Thornton (Chellow) YD
 1521 Thomas Thornton (Denby Hall) WYR
 1545 Richard Thornton (Thornton) SR

Threapleton, Threappleton, Thrippleton

These uncommon Bradford surnames have always been something of a mystery: they suggest a place-name origin and yet no obvious source exists. The fact is that they are variants of Threapland and have outlived the original form of the name. It is not exactly clear how they developed, but the change occurred in the 18th century and has a direct parallel in cases such as Strickland/Strickleton; Frankland/Frankleton. A field-name 'Threapleton' in Wyke shows the same development from 'Threapelandes'. In Old English the word 'threap' meant 'to dispute' and it is a common prefix in minor place-names, presumably being used when the ownership was in question. There is a village of Threapland, near Cracoe in Wharfedale, but as the early history of the Bradford surname is in Allerton cum Wilsden it may in this case derive from a lost locality.

c 1200 Thomas de Threpeland (Allerton) EYCh
 1361 John de Trepelande (Bradford) CR
 1459 John Threapland (Wilsden) Th 2
 1524 Thomas Threpland (Allerton) SR
 1672 Joseph Threapland (Calverley) PR
 1707-11 Joseph Threapland/Threbelton (Guiseley) PR

Tillotson

'Son of Tillot', a diminutive of Matilda via the pet form Till. It is apparently a surname with a single origin, the progenitor being Tillot de Northwod who lived in Cowling, in Kildwick parish (1379). The surname ramified in Kildwick and its neighbour Carleton in the 16th century and is still common there. It probably arrived in Bradford in the early 1600s.

 1379 John Tillotson (Cowling) PTY
 1510 Pers Tyllotson (Cowling) MR
 1621 Thomas Tillotson (Kildwick) PR
 1641 John Tillitson (Clayton) Prot R

Tommis See Thomas

Tong, Tonge

There are places named Tong or Tonge in several English counties, but the Bradford surname is derived from the local Tong. This village is situated on a prominent ridge and the name refers to this position, although opinions differ as to the precise etymology. The family was of some standing originally but had declined considerably in status and numbers by the 17th century.

c 1200 Richard de Tong. Th 6
 1360 John de Tonge (Eccleshill) WCR
 1431 John Tonge (Calverley) YD
 1539 Nicholas Tong (Manningham) MR
 1614 Thomas Tonge (Manningham) WYR

Toothill, Tootill, Tottle, Tuthill, Tutill, Tuttle

This is a common minor place-name, signifying 'look-out hill', and the surname is likely to have several origins. One family derived its name from Toothill in Rastrick, but there is no explicit link with Toothills living in the Haworth area in the early 1500s. One possible connection might be through the Leventhorpes, who held the so-called manor of Toothill in the early 1400s and who, like the Toothills of Rastrick, had branches in the south of England.

1255 Richard de Totil (Rastrick) YD
1379 John de Tutill (Rastrick) PTY
1481 Thomas Totehill (Rastrick)WCR
1530 Edmund Tutyll (Haworth)WYR
1641 Joseph Tootill (Haworth)Prot R

Tordoff, Torday

This surname arrived in Bradford and Leeds in the 16th century and survived in Wibsey, which has been its main 'home' for over 400 years. It is clear that the final consonant was not pronounced colloquially for a deposition in the Quarter Sessions refers in 1680 to 'Robert Torder as hee calls himselfe' and this explains the variants found in the parish registers. The origin and meaning of the surname have been the subject of much speculation, especially as some branches of the family cling to a belief that Scotland was their original home. The two main stories have been given little credence for they differ considerably in detail and in each case relate to events long after the initial settlement. Moreover it seems reasonably certain that the immediate ancestors of the Wibsey family lived in York as pewterers. For the years before that, however, there is a complete lack of information in English sources and one possible explanation is that the York family had indeed migrated from Scotland, directly or indirectly. Certainly 'Tordoff' occurs as a by-name in Dumfriesshire in the 13th century. The likely source in that case would be Torduff Point on the Solway Firth, a place-name of Gaelic origin (i.e. hill-black). It would however be amazing if a tradition of a Scottish origin had survived for so long and it seems more probable that William Tordoff of York was a recent arrival in the city in the 1490s and gave the name of his place of origin as his surname. The fact that Scottish surnames stabilised so much later than English surnames would support this view.

1296 John de Dordofe (Dornock) Black
1499 William Tordofft (York) FY
1524 Cuthbert Turduff (York) SR
1572 Robert Tordoffe (Wibsey) WYD
1614-23 William Tordoffe/Tordey (Bradford) PR

Tuthill, Tutill, Tuttle See Toothill

Varey, Varah, Varo See also Virr

Reaney said of these surnames that they were 'clearly a late development of Farrow', and drew his examples from 18th century Suffolk sources. Locally, however, the surname first occurred c1640 at Adwalton in Birstall parish and it was spelt in a wide variety of ways. The origin and meaning are not clear, but there are similar surnames in the 16th century in South Yorkshire and Nottinghamshire. The substitution of initial 'V' for 'F' would be very unusual in the West Riding so these names may have a different origin to the one suggested by Reaney, possibly outside the county.

1566-75 Richard Varay/Vayray/Veyrie (Rotherham) YF
1640-77 William Varay/Varah/Varo (Adwalton) Birstall PR
1674-76 Edward Varey/Varah (East Bierley) Birstall PR

Verity, Varty (?)

Prolific now in Bradford. Much of its ramification centred on North Bierley, where it has a history of some 350 years. Although these Veritys seem likely to have links with Veritys living in Linton in Craven in the 1560s the earlier history of both families is still obscure. In neither case is there an obvious link with early examples of similar surnames in Leeds, Ripon, York and Bowland. It is possible, as Reaney has shown, that the surname could derive from the abstract noun 'verity', possibly as a nickname for the man who played the part of Verity in a medieval play, but this origin still has to be proved.

1293 William Veryte (Leeds) YAJ 13
1393 John Verty (Calverley) Th 6
1483 Edmund Verty (York) FY
1524 Isabel Vertee (York) SR
1566 Lancelot Veritie (Linton) PR
1638 Cuthbert Verity (Bierley) PR

Vickers

The vicar's servant. It has numerous origins but no obvious one locally. There were families in Tong and Northowram in 1545 and the surname was common in Bradford a century later.

1379 John 'seruiens Vicarii' (Leeds) PTY
1483 William Wekers (sic) (Ovenden) YD
1521 James Vicars (Ovenden) WYR
1545 John Vecars (Northowram) SR
1597 Robert Vickers (Bradford) PR

Virr

Well established now in Bradford. It is first recorded in Tong in the 1660s but its origin is uncertain. It may be a variant of Varey which appeared in the same area at roughly the same time.

1663 Peter Varr/Ver (Tong) Birstall PR
1694 Peter Virr (Tong) Tempest
1717 Joseph Virr (Bradford) PR

Waddington

From Waddington (i.e. Wada's farmstead), a township in Bowland. The surname is recorded from the 12th century and was prominent in Waddington itself. It reached Bradford as early as 1539 but did not ramify there immediately. Now however it is prolific and well distributed in the West Riding generally.

1283 Walter de Wadington (Rimington) YI
1379 Thomas de Wadyngton (Waddington) PTY
1438 William Wadington (Thornton in Craven) YAS 133
1539 William Wadyngton (Bowling) MR
1641 William Waddington (Wilsden) Prot R

Wade

From 'Wada', an Old English personal name (see Reaney). The surname is prolific and widely distributed and probably has numerous origins. There are several references to it in Bradford in the 1400s and early 1500s but they are not obviously connected and may have originated in places such as Sowerbyshire or Wharfedale where the name was also well established.

1284 Juliana Wade (Sowerby) WCR
1350 Hugh Wade (Sowerby) WCR
1414 William Wade (Bradford) CR
1488 George Wade (Bradford) WYR
1539 William Wade (Allerton) MR

Wadsworth

From Wadsworth (i.e. Wæddi's enclosure), a township near Heptonstall. The main ramification of the surname was initially in the Calder valley and later in the Huddersfield area, but the township of Wadsworth shares a common boundary with Hawowth and the surname is recorded there from an early date. This name should not be confused with Wadsworth/Wordsworth in South Yorkshire.

1274 Adam de Waddeswrth
(Sowerby) WCR
1343 John de Waddesworth
(Bradford) CR
1539 Robert Waddyswurthe
(Haworth) MR

Walker
The regional term for a cloth fuller,
i.e. the man in charge of the 'walk
miln'. It has multiple origins and was
already prolific in 1545.
1342 William Walker, 'in charge of the
fulling-mill' (Bradford) BAS
1379 Thomas Walker, fuller
(Bradford) PTY
1446 John Walker (Bierley) BAS
1545 John Walker (Bradford) SR

A Rastrick family took its name from
the locality 'Wolfker' (i.e. wolf-marsh)
and this probably became Walker also.
1348 Richard del Wolfker (Rastrick)
WCR
1440 Robert Woleker (Rastrick) WCR
1505 Christopher Walker (Rastrick)
WCR
1545 Brian Wolker (Halifax) PR

Ward
Usually for a 'ward' or watchman. The
surname had numerous origins and was
widely distributed in Yorkshire by the
end of the 14th century.
1298 Adam le Ward (Holme) WCR
1379 Matilda Ward (Shipley) PTY
1422 Geoffrey Warde (Bradford) CR
1524 Miles Ward (Bradford) SR
1545 Thomas Ward (Bradford) SR

Wardman
It probably has a single family origin
in Yorkshire and means literally 'the
servant of a man named Ward'. It is
first found in Embsay and by the early
1500s was well established in and
around Skipton. It may have reached
Bradford from there or from Arthing-
ton Grange where Richard Wardman
was taxed in 1545.

1379 William Ward; William Wardman (Embsay) PTY
1522 Antony Wardeman (Skipton)
LB
1620 John Wardman (Horton) WYR

Waterhouse
In the 14th century most of the references to Waterhouse locate the surname in the Colne valley and the
evidence suggests that it derives from
a settlement there, close to the river,
probably in the Crimble area. In the
15th century, however, it became very
common in Skircoat and Warley, some
distance away, but also in the manor
of Wakefield. (One branch even had
interests in Lincolnshire in 1424, a
fact which lead some genealogists to
think it may have originated there.)
It was not long before Waterhouse
found its way into the Bradford area
and in his will of 1533 John Waterhouse of Skircoat referred to a kinsman
and namesake in Idle.
1317 Simon of the Watirhous
(Golcar) WCR
1397 Adam de Waterhowse
(Slaithwaite) MD/335
1484 Richard Waterhouse (Warley)
WYR
1545 John Waterhous (Idle) SR

Watman, Whatman
These names can be variants of Watmough.
1569 John Watman/Watmough
(Halifax) PR
1676-79 William Watmough/Whatman
(Liversedge) PR

Watmore, Whatmore, Whatmoor
See also **Watman**
These rare surnames can be variants of
Watmough in Yorkshire c.f. Ellis-
mough.
1541 William Watmore (Halifax) YD
1568-78 Charles Watmore/Richard
Watmough (Tuxford) WYR

Watmough, Watmuff, Whatmough, Whatmuff

There is no evidence that Robert Watmaghe, who was living in Horton in Ribblesdale in the 14th century, had any descendants locally, nor that he is connected in any way with a family of the same name recorded in parts of East Lancashire from c1400. Clearly though the Horton family could have moved the relatively short distance to the Burnley area where the surname is said to have been well established in the mid 1400s (McKinley). In any case the name probably means 'Walter's kinsman' and can be compared with Ellismough and Muff. There are isolated examples of the surname in the West Riding in the 1500s e.g. Normanton (1535) and Halifax (1539) but it was in Bradford that it eventually ramified successfully and the links there with Lancashire are often more explicit: property in Allerton in 1634, for example, was held by Joshua Watmough of London, a younger son of Hugh Watmough of Bury (WYD). This may mean that John Watmough's purchase of houses in Thornton in 1572 referred to Thornton in Bradforddale, although Thornton in Craven is more likely (YF).

    1557 William Wattmoughe (Halifax) PR
    1669 William Watmough (Liversedge) PR

Webster

Prolific and widely distributed. In Old English it was the feminine form of the word for a weaver but in the 14th century, when such occupational terms were becoming hereditary surnames, it applied to men. It had multiple origins and in the 14th century there were Websters in Eccleshill, Calverley and Bingley.

    1349 John Webster (Bradford) CR

    1468 John Webster (Bradford) YD
    1539 John Webster (Bradford) MR

Whaley

Possibly from Whaley, the name of places in Derbyshire and Cheshire. However, the local evidence suggests that it is also a variant of Whalley.

    1608 Alice Whaley (Stanbury) WYR
    1764 Benjamin Whaley/Walley (Leeds) PR

Whalley See also Whaley

From Whalley (i.e. hill-clearing), a Lancashire parish which included part of Bowland. The surname is recorded in Yorkshire from the early 13th century and was present in Halifax and York in the 1300s. It became established much later in Leeds and Bradford and these families probably had more direct links with Bowland.

         by Bowland) PTY
    1482 William Whalley (Gisburn) YAS 133
    1522 William Walley (Bracewell) LB
    1561 William Whalley (Leeds) WYR
    1641 Michael Whalley (Wilsden) Prot R

Whatman See Watman

Whatmore See Watmore

Whatmough, Whatmuff See Watmough

Whitaker, Whittaker

A prolific but complicated surname which has been well established in Bradford since the 14th century. It clearly derives from a place-name, but the exact settlement has not been identified, possibly because it was depopulated c1350. Smith lists an undocumented White Acres in Clayton which conceivably is the locality mentioned in a charter of c1200. (This was confirmation by Roger de Lacy of a grant of lands to Byland Abbey and amongst those listed were Clayton, Allerton, Crossley, Wilsden and 'Wyth-acris', a spelling very similar to the early surname forms.) Unfortunately these Bradford Whitakers cannot yet be linked with families of the same name in Huddersfield and Lower Ribblesdale, also well evidenced from the 14th century. The picture is further complicated by the ramification of a Lancashire family which lived at High Whitaker and established links with families in the Bradford area.

1342 John Whitacre (Bradford) CR
1379 Roger Whitteacres (Thornton) PTY
1412 Thomas Qwytakyrs (Allerton) CR
1524 Thomas Whyttaker (Haworth) SR
1545 James Whetecars (Haworth) SR

Whiteley, Whitley

The place-name occurs several times in the West Riding, but there is no obvious local origin for the surname either in Bradford or in Sowerby, which is probably where the first Bradford Whiteleys came from. In the 13th and 14th centuries the name is recorded over a relatively wide area and in at least one case derived from Lower or Upper Whitley, near Kirkheaton. However, there is nothing to connect this family directly with one which later ramified successfully in Rishworth, or indeed with families living in 1545 in Northowram, Pudsey and Bingley.

1298 Richard de Wyteley (Sowerby) WCR
1352 Richard del Whitlygh (Sowerby) WCR
1421 John Whitley (Bradford) CR
1539 John Whitteley (Bradford) MR

Wibsey

Although it was never a prolific surname Wibsey was recorded at regular intervals in Yorkshire for a period of about three hundred years. It was actually relatively numerous at the time of the Poll Tax, occurring in North Bierley (2), Cleckheaton (1), and Adwick (1), and even in 1545 there were three families taxed, one of them in Haworth. It may survive elsewhere in England or even overseas, but was last recorded in Yorkshire in the 17th century.

1366 John de Websay (Hunsworth) CR
1424 John Wibsey (East Bierley) Th 6
1545 George Wibsey (Gomersal) SR
1656 Richard Wibsey (Hartshead) PR

Widdop, Widdup

From Widdop (i.e. wide valley) a locality in Wadsworth. Branches of the family had moved over into Airedale by c1500.

1379 Agnes filia Willelmi (Haworth) Thomas filius Willelmi (Thornton) PTY
1492 Robert Wedope (Wadsworth) Clay
1539 Richard Wedop (Thornton) MR
1645 Edmond Widdop (Wibsey) WYR

Wilkinson

'Son of Wilkin', a diminutive of William via the pet form Will. It has several West Riding origins and locally there were numerically important families in Elland and Ovenden.

1379 Agnes filia Willelmi (Haworth) Thomas filius Willelmi (Thornton) PTY
1414 Adam Wylkynson (Haworth) CR
1488 William Wilkynson (Haworth) YD
1545 Richard Wilkynson (Bradford) SR

Willman, Wilman

The first of the name in Bradford was a Wilsden man with the unusual Christian name Rainbrown. It was clearly a significant choice of name for it was borne by generations of Wilmans, and it suggests therefore a close link with Rainbrown Bolling of Bradford, who married Alice Philip in 1491. Where the Wilsden family came from is not certain, but Wilman at this time was a variant of Wildman, and a family of this name had been established in the area between Clapham and Horton in Ribblesdale for over 150 years. Wildman was probably a nickname initially.

1379 William Wyldman (Clapham) PTY
1406 John Wyldeman (Clapham) YI
1522 John Wyldman/Thomas Wylman (Horton in Ribblesdale) LB
1539 Raynbrowne Willman (Wilsden) MR
1542 John Wylman of Bradford, Halifax PR

Alternatively, in common with other families, the Wilmans may have moved into the area from York where the surname was well known. Here too it could have been a variant of Wildman, but there is some evidence pointing to a derivation from the Norman personal name 'Willemin'. See Reaney, p. 136.

c 1300 Roger filius Wylman (Guisborough) SS
1379 William Wylman (Selby) PTY
1475 Laurence Wildeman (York) WYR
1508 Robert Wilman (York) FY

Wilson

'Son of Will', a pet form of William. It has multiple origins and these appear to include at least two locally.

1394 Robert Wilson (Pudsey) YD
1484 Thomas Wilson (Pudsey) WYD
1545 John Wilson (Pudsey) SR

1342 Adam Willeson (Bradford) BAS
1412 John Wilson (Manningham) CR
1539 William Wilson (Manningham) MR

Woabank See Obank

Wood

Most townships still had areas of uncleared woodland in the Middle Ages and 'de Wode' became a common surname as the population increased in the period before 1350. It had multiple origins therefore and by 1545 there were Woods in over thirty villages close to Bradford. One family lived in Bierley, but there were successful ramifications in several places, including Halifax and Birstall.

1307 Hugh de Wodde (Bierley) WYD
1379 John de Wode (North Bierley) PTY
1545 Robert Wood (North Bierley) SR

Wooler, Wooller

Probably from Wooler in Northumberland. The surname is first recorded in the commercial centres of York and Ripon, but a family living in Airedale was probably responsible for the modest ramification in Bradford.

1370 David de Wollore (Ripon) SS
1430 John Wollore (York) FY
1446 John Wollour (Kildwick) WYR
1511 Henry Woller (Cowling) MR
1545 John Woller (Bingley) SR
1641 John Wooler (Bradford) Prot R

Worsman See also Worsnop

From Wolstenholme, a locality in Rochdale parish. The surname is recorded in the Calder valley from the 14th century but was slow to ramify. This variant, which is a metathesised form of Worsnam, seems to be peculiar to Bradford.

1386 Robert de Wolstonholme (Sowerby) WCR
1461 Thomas Wolstonholme (Sowerby) WCR
1570 John Worssnhoume (Halifax) PR
1627 Thomas Worsnam (Bradford) PR
1716 Isaac Worsman (Tong) QS

Worsnop, Worsnup See also Worsman

A variant of Worsnam, which derives from Wolstenholme in Lancashire. It was not at all unusual for a final 'm' to interchange with a final 'p' c.f. 1615 Jane Mossom/Mossopp (Beverley) WYR. Occasional examples of this variant occur in Halifax, but it was principally in Birstall and Tong that the name finally stabilised.

1591 Richard Woorsnope (Halifax) PR
1750 Jane Worsnop alias Worsman (Tong) Tempest
1782 William Worsnop (Wyke) PR

Wright

A carpenter or woodworker. It has several West Riding origins, including one in Bowling, but for a long time it was not particularly prolific in Bradford.

1379 John le Wryght (Bowling) PTY
1463 John Wryght (Bowling) WYD
1545 Humphrey Wright (Bowling) SR

Wrose

The Shipley place-name is said to mean 'a knot, something twisted', (Smith) and to refer to the steep-sided hill on which the village stands. The surname had a long history in the Calverley area, where Wrose and Wrosse were alternative spellings. Although it is no longer found with initial 'W', it would not be surprising if it survived occasionally as Rose and Ross, although both of these have alternative origins.

1342 Amabilla del Wros (Bradford) CR
1475 Robert Wrosse (Pudsey) CR
1545 Robert Wrose (Bramley) SR
1669 Nicholas Wroose (Otley) PR
1708 Jonathan Ross (Calverley) PR

Yeadall, Yeadell See also Yeadon, Yewdall

These surnames developed when Yewdall arrived in that part of Airedale where Yeadon was already well established. The suffixes 'den' and 'dale' were often interchanged in both placenames and surnames and Yeadon was no doubt assumed to be a name in the same category.

1556 Thomas Yedall (Kirkstall) WYR
1579-84 Hugh Yeadall/Udall (Windhill) PR; BAS
1638-43 Walter Yeadall/Yeadon (Idle) PR

Yeadon

A prolific surname concentrated in the Bradford/Leeds area. It derives from Yeadon, a township in Guiseley parish, and is first recorded in the 12th century. There was almost certainly some confusion with Yewdall.

1379 John de Yedon (Yeadon) PTY
1459 Richard Yeadon (Yeadon) Th 2
1545 Christopher Yedon (Yeadon) SR
1641 Richard Yeadon (Bradford) Prot R

Yewdall

Probably from Yewdale in North Lancashire. Members of one family, starting with John Yowdale de Borodale (1456), held the office of bailiff for Fountains Abbey until the Dissolution. Alice Yowdall was taxed in Malham in 1379 and part of this township was held by Fountains so the link may go back even further. The surname was also recorded in York from 1477-1669, with a range of spellings from Yudalle and Yowdall to Udall. Now, Yewdall is essentially a Leeds/ Bradford name and its history there appears to date from Elizabeth's reign when a family settled in Windhill.

1584-1604 Hugh Udale/Yewdall (Windhill) BAS; WYR

1641 John Yudall/Michael Udall (Dewsbury) Prot R

1719 Thomas Yewdall (Bradford) PR

ABBREVIATIONS

BAS	*The Bradford Antiquary*, A Journal of the Bradford Historical and Antiquarian Society, published in three series. An index to the contents is held in Bradford Central Library in the Local History Department.
Black	G.F. Black, *Surnames of Scotland*.
Clay	J.W. Clay, Halifax Wills, 1389-1544, Privately printed.
CR	Court Rolls. Eight volumes of Bradford court rolls have been transcribed and are held in the Central Library i.e. 1338-1362; 1410-1414; 1420-22; 1569-1579; 1601/2; 1625-29; 1662-66; 1690; 1695/6. Yeadon court rolls have been transcribed for 1361-1476 by S. Whittle, and privately published by G.R. Price (1984). See also WCR.
.Dodsworth	Extracts from the work of Roger Dodsworth have been published in the *Yorkshire Archaeological Journal*.
EYCh.	W. Farrer, C.T. Clay, *Early Yorkshire Charters*, 10 vols.
FA	W.T. Lancaster, *Cartulary of Fountains Abbey*, 2 vols.
Fishwick	H. Fishwick, *History of the Parish of Rochdale*.
FY	Register of the Freemen of York, 1272-1760, 2 vols. (SS).
HAS	*Halifax Antiquarian Society Transactions*.
Hoyle	R. Hoyle, *Lord Thanet's Benefaction to the Poor of Craven in 1685*, Privately printed 1978.
HT	Hearth Tax Returns. Those for Leeds and Skyrack Wapentake have been published by the Thoresby Society, and that for Tong in the Yorkshire County Magazine.
KM	Kirklees Muniments, i.e. the Papers of the Armytage family, held in the archives at Calderdale Central Library, Halifax, and in process of classification. An earlier printed catalogue is available.
LB	Transcribed by R. Hoyle in Yorkshire Arch. Soc., Record Series, Vol. CXLV.
MD 335	A collection of early deeds held at 'Claremont', Leeds, the Headquarters of the Yorkshire Arch. Soc. and part of the West Yorkshire Archive Service.
Misc. Mss.	A collection of deeds held in the Bradford archives at 15, Canal Road.
MR	Muster Rolls. The roll for Bradford and district is in BAS Vol. I. The date 1539 is not certain to be accurate. The roll of 1510 for Craven and district has most recently been published in YAS, Vol. CXLV.
NC	J.H. Turner (ed), *The Nonconformist Register*.
PC	*The Plumpton Correspondence*, Camden Soc., Vol. IV.
PR	Parish Register.
Prot R	The Protestation Returns (1641), held in the House of Lords Record Office. A transcription of the Bradford lists is in BAS, New Series, 1982 but it contains some mistakes.
PTY	Returns of the Poll Tax for the West Riding, 1379, YAS.
QS	The Quarter Sessions Records of the West Riding of Yorkshire, held in the West Yorkshire Archive Service Headquarters, Wakefield. i.e. Indictment Books, Order Books and Rolls.
Reaney	P.H. Reaney, *A Dictionary of British Surnames*. 1961.
Smith	A.H. Smith, *Place-names of the West Riding of Yorkshire*, 8 vols.

SR	Subsidy Rolls. Those for Craven are in YAS CXLV, those for Morley wapentake (1524) in YAJ, Vol. II and (1545, 1588) in Th. IX and XI.
SS	Publications of the Surtees Society. (Where important the volume number is given.)
Tempest	The Papers of the Tempests of Tong, held in the Bradford archives.
Th	Publications of the Thoresby Society. (Where important the volume number is given.)
TN	The Temple Newsam Collection of Deeds, held in the Leeds archives, Sheepscar.
VHL	*The Victoria County History of Lancashire.*
WB	The Papers of the Beaumonts of Whitley, held in the archives, Kirklees Central Library, Huddersfield.
WCR	Wakefield Court Rolls. These are held at 'Claremont', Leeds, West Yorks. Archive Service, but two series have been published: 1274-1331, YAS Record Series, 5 vols and 1331-33; 1348-50; 1350-52; 1583-85; 1639-40; 1664-65, YAS Wakefield Court Rolls Series.
Weston	The Weston Deeds, held at 'Claremont', Leeds, West Yorks. Archive Service.
WPB	W.P. Baildon, *Baildon and the Baildons.*
WYAS	*West Yorkshire: an Archaeological Survey to A.D. 1500.* 3 vols.
WYD	*West Yorkshire Deeds*, Local Record Series, Bradford Historical and Antiquarian Soc.
WYR	*Index of Wills in the York Registry* 1389-1688, YAS, 15 vols.
YAJ	*The Yorkshire Archaeological Journal.*
YAS	The Yorkshire Archaeological Society, Record Series.
YD	*Yorkshire Deeds*, YAS, 10 vols.
YF	*Yorkshire Fines*, YAS, 11 vols.
Y Gen.	*The Yorkshire Genealogist.*
YI	*Yorkshire Inquisitions*, YAS, 5 vols.
Y Pipe	Publications of the 'Pipe' Roll Society.